FAITH-FORMING
JUNIOR HIGH MINISTRY

Beyond Pizza 101

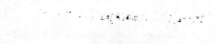

Foreword by Duffy Robbins

FAITH-FORMING JUNIOR HIGH MINISTRY

Beyond Pizza 101

Drew A. Dyson

Faith-Forming Junior High Ministry:
Beyond Pizza 101

#51756198

03 04 05 06 07 08 09 10 11 12—10 9 8 7 6 5 4 3 2 1

MANUFACTURED IN THE UNITED STATES OF AMERICA

Dedication

In loving memory of David Justin Agnew and TJ Stockdale

Acknowledgments

Many people come into our lives that embody the grace of God. My life has been blessed by many people who have dared to show me God's love at the most vulnerable times and places. I especially want to thank my wife, Diane for the grace and love she has shown me every single day over the last 9 years. My children, Allison and Jeremy, have transformed my life and taught me the true essence of unconditional love. My parents, Mollie and Ron, have struggled with me through many difficult times yet continued to love me.

I want to thank those people who had the courage to minister to a hurting, rebellious teenager even when I tried to make it impossible—Dale Irvin, Rich and Gina Hendrickson, Mike Badger, Walter Quiqq, and many others.

My ministry has been shaped by many people who have taught me, shepherded me, challenged me, and pastored me. I especially want to thank the youth, parents, staff, and volunteer youth workers of the United Methodist Churches in Bridgewater, Ocean Grove, and Middletown, New Jersey. You may never know how much your lives have shaped mine. I have also had the privilege of learning from two of the best youth ministry educators—Kenda Creasy Dean and Duffy Robbins—whose friendship and mentoring are invaluable.

Finally, I want to thank those whose passion and commitment to junior high youth ministry have helped give shape to this book. Throughout these pages you will find the incredible witness and insights of some of the best junior high ministers and youth that I know—Jim Bielefeldt, Elizabeth Bielinski, Gabriella Graziano, Lynne Wells Graziano, Susan Hay, and Kara Lassen-Oliver. I also want to thank Jenny Youngman and the editorial staff of the United Methodist Publishing House for their guidance and encouragement on this project.

Contents

Foreword

The Darkroom Principle

By Duffy Robbins

He was relatively new in youth ministry. I had known him for just over two years, but I had already come to respect his desire to be used of God, and to do whatever he did with excellence for Christ. That is, no doubt, why I was so moved as he painted for me a picture of his "rookie season" in youth ministry—a season marked by fouls, strike outs, balls, and games that got "rained out." After a year or more of finding little success in youth ministry, a year in which he often gave his best effort with little or no encouragement from those who oversaw his work, he was just about ready to toss in the towel.

> *Real answers do not come so easily.*

Anyone in youth ministry knows those feelings. I surely have experienced the threat of burn out from time to time. If you are reading this book with more than two weeks of youth ministry experience, you may be thinking that this youth worker's story sounds like your own. And, perhaps, it is.

Youth ministry is hard work. There's no escaping the hard work. More often than not, ironically, it's not the youth themselves who make the work so difficult. The difficulties can come from all around—unsupportive pastors, boards that want to see quick results, and parents who view an entire ministry through the lens of their own child. Wouldn't it be nice if every youth ministry issue could be solved with a new three-step approach or an exciting new strategy diagram or a catchy on-the-edge programming idea? But, as Drew Dyson reminds us in FAITH-FORMING JUNIOR HIGH MINISTRY, real answers do not come so easily. What I shared with my youth worker friend that day is what I think may be one of the most encouraging principles I've learned in all my years of youth ministry. I call it "The Darkroom Principle."

A good friend of mine really enjoys photography. Unlike the "shoot and ship" approach that I'm accustomed to—shooting the pictures and then shipping them off to the camera store for processing—he develops his own photographs in his own darkroom, doing the creative work in a small basement hideaway where the major feature is darkness or dim light. He carefully dips the undeveloped photographs into several different chemicals so that they will develop properly when exposed to the light. It's a delicate process, painstaking (or so it seems to me) because there was no shortcut through it.

A few days after my first tour through his dark room, I began to gain a new appreciation for how God often works in life and ministry. That tour helped me see that it often takes a dark place to bring out the light in a picture.

> *We need to be reminded that sometimes God's most precious pictures are developed in darkness.*

One of the most challenging elements of real-life middle school ministry is that we spend a lot of time working in God's darkroom, patiently waiting on God to do what only God can do. The very nature of ministry with junior high youth is being in a place where the photograph is not fully developed. I've often thought that middle school ministry feels like taking a picture with an old Polaroid™ camera and watching with expectation to see how the picture would turn out. I can remember waving the photo around and blowing on it, trying to speed up the process. I was eager to see the image develop.

Ministry with junior high youth can often feel as if we've been waving and blowing for months without seeing the picture we're expecting to see. There will be students for whom the picture looks blurry, distorted—not at all like the image of Christ we had been praying and hoping for. But the process cannot be rushed. And the process will sometimes make us feel as if we're the ones who have been left in the dark.

Because we usually want to see instant results, we need to be reminded that sometimes God's most precious pictures are developed in darkness. Perhaps that is why David wrote in Psalm 19:2, "Day to day pours forth speech, and night to night declares knowledge." David was a man whose own process of development knew more than its share of darkness. And yet, it may have been those times of darkness that taught him the lessons he simply could not have learned in times of light.

Daylight brought lots of speech. Darkness brought knowledge. We may not hear as much in the darkness, but what we do hear is often vitally important to our growth. Many of the great saints of the church talk about how their own spiritual development was marked by a "dark night of the soul" (St. John of the Cross) and how it brought them to a new depth spiritually.

Does understanding this principle make junior high ministry easier? No. But it does give us a better appreciation of the fact that only God sees the big picture—and that nurturing middle school disciples is a long stage in the process of development. The process surely begins with exposure to the Light. But it often cannot proceed without patient (and painstaking) exposure to the dark.

> *We may not hear as much in the darkness, but what we do hear is often vitally important to our growth.*

In *Mere Christianity*, C.S. Lewis captures that ungainly process of development with a reflection on why God became human. He contends that the reason for God's coming in human flesh was not just to bring about a better version but an altogether *new* kind of person. To make his point, Lewis tells a story of a horse that grew wings—not a horse that learned to jump higher and farther, but a horse that actually became a winged creature. The horse with wings could surpass even the highest jumps of a regular horse. However, in the beginning, while the wings were still growing and developing, the horse was awkward and had lumps on its shoulders. From the outside no one knew that the horse was becoming something different, but something was certainly happening. The horse was changing into something new and amazing.

Sometimes junior high youth will appear awkward, and we won't necessarily see the changes that are taking place. However, we can be sure that God is working behind the scenes to cause our young people to soar higher than we ever thought possible.

What a wonder that God, who brought all creation into being with the words, "Let there be light . . . ," would flash across the marred face of humanity the light of life, the light of the world, the light of Jesus. And then, more wonderful still, that by exposure to God's light, middle school students could become new creatures, and could step out of darkness into life. What we see now in that junior high kid is only a hint of what is to come. The image is blurred; it's faint; the colors are bland. But, with careful handling and the proper exposure to light, that image is destined one day to look like Jesus.

> *By exposure to God's light, middle school students could become new creatures, and could step out of darkness into life.*

I am so grateful for people like you who care enough about Jesus to care about junior high students. I am grateful as well to Drew Dyson for writing this truthful, thoughtful book about junior high ministry. The book's combination of theological conviction and common sense reminds us that developing a ministry with junior high youth is about much more than snap and flash. Every chapter speaks with the voice of one who has spent some time in that darkroom, who has waved and blown and waited for that picture to develop, watching to see junior highs more truly bear the likeness of Jesus. I welcome this book and its hopeful, realistic approach.

As I said to my young youth ministry comrade, all of us who work with teenagers will face times of discouragement in ministry. Not only do we not see the big picture, sometimes the picture we do see does not provide much hope. But youth ministry is all about the development process. We must never underestimate the power of Light that works even in the darkest of rooms.

And never judge the final picture by looking at the negatives.

Enjoy FAITH-FORMING JUNIOR HIGH MINISTRY, and thanks for your ministry!

— **Duffy Robbins**
Associate Professor of Youth Ministry,
Eastern University,
St. Davids, Pennsylvania

Day to day pours forth speech, and night to night declares knowledge.
(Psalm 19:2)

Introduction

The Messy World of Junior High Ministry

I couldn't imagine where they were all coming from. Certainly I had seen several of them before, but most of them were new faces. As they walked in, they greeted me and the other leaders politely and went immediately to the game room to await the start of the meeting. Student leaders mingled with new people and several students gathered in the corner to pray for the ministry in the coming year. This was the moment I was waiting for all summer—the kick-off meeting of the junior high ministry at my new church.

The meeting began exactly on time with words of welcome, announcements, and several ice breakers led by students. The crowd of hundreds was enthusiastic and focused. I could feel the energy as the Holy Spirit filled the jam-packed youth room. The band began to play up-tempo songs of praise leading to softer songs of worship. With great excitement and anticipation, I climbed the stairs to the stage and began my message. It was unbelievable, if I do say so myself. The youth laughed at every joke, they cried at every story. Believe it or not, they even read along with the Scripture from the Bibles that they brought from home! After a personal story told through choked-back tears, I was ready to "bring it all home" with a call for personal commitment. Just as I heard the words come out of my mouth, "every head bowed, every eye closed," it happened...RING...RING ...RING...RING! The alarm clock went off.

"Honey, wake up! Youth group starts in less than an hour and you don't want to be late on the first night." Ugh! I must have fallen asleep watching the golf tournament on television. It was 4:15 on Sunday afternoon and I had to get out of the house and get to the church for youth group. As you can imagine, the "real" meeting went a little differently.

At 5:05, only two youth were at the church talking with our ten adult leaders. We delayed the start of our meeting while we waited for the other students to arrive. Finally at 5:20, I gave some announcements and opened the meeting in prayer, which, of course, was interrupted by some incessant giggling. The game that I had been planning for weeks that was going to be the perfect ice breaker flopped. I had to repeat the directions four times and still nobody got it. To top it off, someone got hurt by running into a closed door.

"Time to move on," I thought. After retrieving some ice from the kitchen, we moved to the sanctuary for a time of praise and worship. As the student band played and sang, not one other student opted to use their vocal cords—they must have been worn out from screaming earlier in the evening. As I got up to deliver a message, I tripped and fell. Once the laughter died out from the fall, there wasn't a peep. Not because I had their attention, but because they didn't get it. The jokes were not funny, apparently. The stories did not connect with the youth. And, I couldn't get my message across clearly.

As I locked up the church later that night, I stopped in the sanctuary to pray. "God, tonight was a mess. I'm sorry that I failed you. I don't know what happened. I had talked to four other people who used that same game and their youth loved it! I worked hard on the message and even committed it to memory. Maybe, I'm not the right person for this ministry. Certainly someone else in the church is more qualified to lead the junior high ministry."

On the way home, I discovered a peaceful assurance. In my mind, I saw the smile on Haley's face as I called her by her name before I even met her. I heard the laughter of the boys in the bathroom talking about how much fun they were having—in spite of the stupid game. Through-out that first year there were many bad games, many misplaced talks, and many misdirected pranks. But, there were also many late-night conversations about faith and life in junior high. There were many times when the group reached out to new members and welcomed strangers. There were many "a-ha" moments in Bible study and many seeds planted.

> *"No Peter, put down the sword and give him his ear back."*
>
> *"John, it doesn't matter who sits in the front. In fact, those in the back seat will be rewarded."*
>
> *"Peter, I know this was a great retreat, but building an altar and staying here for the rest of our lives is not an option."*

Indeed, junior high ministry often appears to be a ministry among youth with split (or multiple) personalities. Within an hour, the same student is likely to make a commitment to Jesus Christ and to make fun of the awkward boy in her class. It is enough to make me wonder why junior high ministry is even necessary. Sometimes it seems that it would be better to wait until youth were just a little older and could think abstractly and discuss faith intelligently.

But then I read the Gospels. I see how Jesus chose a group of disciples whose behavior was often similar to many of the junior highs I have worked with. "No Peter, put down the sword and give him his ear back." "John, it doesn't matter who sits in the front. In fact, those in the back seat will be rewarded." "Peter, I know this was a great retreat, but building an altar and staying here for the rest of our lives is not an option." The disciples definitely didn't like the games (note the grumbling about the "pass the fish" game). Most of the time, they didn't understand what Jesus was talking about (see any parable or the Last Supper). Despite their chronological ages, they were not able to think abstractly and, most of the time, did not speak intelligently about faith. The disciples, too, were often saying one thing at one moment and doing something contrary the next (note Peter's statement of faith and subsequent denial).

Yet, through all of these seeming failures, Jesus continued to love, guide, and plant seeds among the disciples. He knew they wouldn't understand until after he was no longer with them—but that was OK.

So Why Junior High Ministry?

Many people consider junior high youth ministry to be one of the most difficult, frustrating ministries in any church. The youth are unpredictable. The results are rarely visible. The accolades are few and far between. However, junior high youth ministry is also one of the most essential ministries in the church of Jesus Christ. Literally, effective junior high ministry is a matter of life and death.

In the first place, early adolescence is a critical time in faith development. A frequently cited study indicates that more than eighty percent of first-time commitments to Jesus Christ happen by the age of fourteen (Barna, *Generation Next*). That does not necessarily mean that when youth commit their life to Christ at junior high camp, they will live as disciples of Christ from that moment on. In fact, most young people that make faith commitments in early adolescence will go through intense periods of questioning, doubt, and denial through their adolescent years and often into adulthood. Statistically, however, if someone is going to make a life-shaping commitment to Jesus Christ, they will make that first decision in early adolescence.

Many junior high ministry programs go between two extremes: a focus on getting youth saved or keeping them in the holding tank. In fairness to junior high youth, they deserve more and are ready to be presented with an opportunity to live their faith and wrestle with tough issues. The balance between choosing Jesus forever and creating a safe place where they can grow and thrive in faith is crucial.

In some places, the focus is on bringing junior high students to a "point of decision" about their eternal future and the rest of their lives. The evangelistic effort in these groups is focused on "getting youth saved".

In most cases, junior high students are not ready or able to understand the eternal implications of the immediate decision forced upon them. In the first place, junior high youth are just beginning to develop decision-making skills. Presenting the gospel in a way that asks young people to make an eternal decision between heaven and hell is not fair or appropriate for early adolescents. That is similar to asking someone who is just learning to ride a motorcycle to perform a jump over 48 burning cars.

In the second place, although they are beginning to develop abstract thinking, most junior high youth are still thinking concretely. When presented with questions of eternal consequence, junior high students will always prefer the safety and comfort of heaven to what they perceive as the fiery pit of eternal damnation.

Finally, junior high students are just beginning to develop their own individual identity. One of the developmental processes of early adolescence is to "try on" various roles to see which one(s) fit them. Junior high students need to be given the freedom and the support in these efforts without being forced into one role.

To say it another way, scaring young people into the faith is not helpful to their long-term spiritual needs. They need to be presented with a choice to choose Jesus every day and to know that no matter how bad life may get, God promises the ultimate peace in heaven. So, before you write that gripping, heart-wrenching sermon for Thursday night at youth camp, consider what it will mean to the youth the following Monday when the youth are with their friends again. Will you present them with a gospel that says "now or never"? Or a gospel that says "walk with Jesus everyday, he knows the way to the Father"?

> *Junior highs need to hear the gospel of Jesus Christ, but more importantly, they need to experience unconditional love, encounter God through people and experiences, and engage their faith through action.*

The other extreme is when churches treat junior high ministry as a "holding tank" to keep youth safe and plugged in to the church until they are ready for more spiritual content. This approach seriously underestimates the spiritual capacity of junior high students and their longing for spiritual connection. Early adolescents need to be presented with the gospel in a manner that is developmentally appropriate in an environment that is safe and nurturing. Junior highs need to hear the gospel of Jesus Christ, but more importantly, they need to experience unconditional love, encounter God through people and experiences, and engage their faith through action.

Junior High Ministry

Beyond being at a pivotal time in spiritual development, early adolescents are just beginning to acquire critical thinking and decision-making skills. As early adolescents venture from the safe nests of childhood to the expansive skies of adulthood, they begin to stretch their own wings by asserting their ability to make decisions for themselves. There was a time when junior high school was indeed a place to nurture those skills so that future decisions would be well thought out. However, in the culture of today's junior high school, early adolescents face daily choices about whether or not to have sex, whether or not to take drugs, which friends to choose, and so on. The decisions that are made by 10, 11 and 12 year olds have the potential to shape the rest of their lives.

The challenge lies in the fact that if we don't get youth in junior high, then we've most likely lost them when they become senior highs. When we focus only on games and parties with junior high youth instead of discipleship, they are not prepared for the more serious faith discussions we throw their way in senior high. Junior highs are not only taking physical shape, but spiritual shape as well. Junior high ministry offers churches an opportunity to walk with early adolescents through the developmental cauldron and be present with young people as they shape their values in the context of a Christian community. When younger youth are nurtured in faith early on, they are more prepared for continued growth and discipleship as they move on to senior high.

So what are appropriate faith commitments for early adolescents? Wayne Rice, noted author and expert in junior high youth ministry, insists that "early adolescents should be taught to make decisions for Christ every day." (*Junior High Ministry*, 27) Junior high youth ministry should not be focused on getting youth to arrive at a final destination, but should provide experiences and situations where young people can make daily decisions about the role of Christ in their lives. As young people develop decision-making skills, they need to learn how to make decisions in light of who they are in Christ. As they shape their identity, they need to fully explore Christian identity as it pertains to all parts of their lives—home, church and school.

Junior high ministry is critical because early adolescents are experiencing startling amounts of fear, hurt and abuse. In order to do effective junior high ministry, we must let go of our sacred images of the carefree, winsome adolescent and realize that many junior high students are dealing with loss, separation, and neglect. By fourteen years of age, most young people have had to deal with one or more of the following: divorced parents, death of a loved one, school violence, poverty, HIV/ AIDS, sexual abuse and/or poverty. Evelyn Parker cites that the greatest danger for young people in this cultural context is the onset of hopelessness that leads to anxiety, despair and in some cases, suicide. Whenever these evils impact the lives of young people, and adults as well, hopelessness lurks. She goes on to say that the church must avoid sidestepping these critical issues to become a place where young people can wrestle with issues of hope and despair and encounter a gracious God who offers hope in the midst of hopelessness. (*Starting Right*, 268)

Unfortunately, much of junior high youth ministry in the church today avoids these complex and painful issues. Those in ministry with junior high youth need to be aware of the critical issues facing junior high students and must be willing to address these issues in the context of Christian community. That is not to say that junior high ministry needs to be serious, issue-based programming. If that were the case, you wouldn't have any junior high youth to worry about. In fact, effective junior high ministry can delicately balance the "egg in the armpit" relay and the difficult issues of violence, poverty, and disease.

What Is "Junior High"?

What is your definition of "junior high"? This is one of the questions that I am asked every time I lead a workshop on junior high ministry. Truthfully, there is no easy answer for who should be included in your junior high ministry program. Without knowing the breakdown of your schools, the content of your children's ministry, or the history of your youth ministry, I cannot give you a clear answer. I can say that for the purpose of writing this book, I have focused on what psychologists refer to as "early adolescents." These young people are typically between the ages of 11 and 14 in sixth through eighth grades. They share common developmental characteristics, needs, and tasks.

School systems pose a difficulty for defining junior high for your church's ministry. If sixth graders in your community are part of the junior high or middle school, it is difficult to exclude them from participating in the junior high ministry. If they attend the grammar school with younger children, it may be better to have them participate in the church's children's ministry with their peers from school. In every junior high ministry that I have led, we have chosen to include sixth graders. We made that decision based not on the school system, because for several years the schools flip-flopped due to class size and space needs, but on the conviction that sixth graders were dealing with many of the same developmental issues as seventh and eighth graders. They are beginning to stretch their wings of independence and rely more heavily on relationships with their peers. They are curious, questioning, and interested. Above all, sixth graders are a ton of fun to be around and open to spiritual influence.

What about "mixed" groups? The question about having mixed groups of senior high and junior high youth is often raised by smaller churches that have fewer than 8 young people in their youth group. First, let me say that it is a joy to have the ability to focus your love and energy on a small group of young people. Do not ever feel that your small youth group is anything less than magnificent. In fact, statistics show that young people from small membership churches are more likely to participate in a church as adults than their counterparts from large youth groups. The primary reason is because young people from smaller groups are plugged in to the full life of the church, not only the youth group. It is much more important to focus on spiritual growth than numerical growth.

That said, I think that you should separate these two age groups whenever possible. Smaller churches that have more than 4 young people in each age group should break them into different groups. The difference in maturity between a sixth grader and an eighth grader is tremendous. The difference between a sixth grader and a twelfth grader is almost insurmountable. Not only are they at different maturity levels, but the issues that they are dealing with are significantly different. A sexuality retreat for junior highs will be significantly different than a sexuality retreat for senior highs. When it is not feasible to have separate groups, I would encourage you to have significant opportunities to divide the two groups for discussion about difficult topics. The most important thing is to be sensitive to the emotional and developmental needs of all of the young people in your ministry.

A Word About This Book

This book is written as an overview of junior high ministry. It is by no means meant to be exhaustive, nor is it meant to replace all of the other outstanding resource materials for junior high youth workers. In the back of the book, I have listed other resources that will be helpful to both inexperienced and veteran junior high workers.

This book is organized into three parts: theology, theory, and practice. In the first part, I ask you to "listen in" on the development of my understanding of the theology of junior high ministry. Practical theology, at its heart, is the norms and practices of ministry that spring from a person's understanding of God. Too often, we have allowed what we teach and understand about God to be shaped by our practice of ministry. Hopefully, this chapter will prompt you to identify your own theological touchstones, wrestle with my concepts, and develop a theology for junior high ministry that will shape all that you do with junior highs.

The second part of the book deals with some of the theoretical work that helps us understand junior high youth. A primer on development covers the physical, emotional, intellectual, social, and spiritual development of early adolescents. Also, you'll find an excellent article on brain development with the newest research on early adolescent development. The section concludes with a look at generational studies focusing on the characteristics of the "Millennial Generation."

The final portion of the book is focused on the practice of junior high ministry. We will look at a holistic understanding of spiritual formation—pulling together the often-separate worlds of worship, prayer, service, and justice and explore junior high leadership development, community building, and educational ministries. The section ends with a look at the needs of adult workers in junior high ministry. I have also included an appendix with my "top 20" list of fun and easy ideas for junior high youth ministry.

As a youth worker, I understand the temptation to jump straight to the practical resources that I can use in my ministry this year, or even this week. However, I want to challenge you to wrestle with your theology for junior high ministry and your understanding of developmental and generational theory *before* you look for the resources to add to your programmatic bag of tricks.

Throughout the book, you will also have the opportunity to hear from different "experts" in junior high ministry. These are people whose wisdom and insight have helped shape my own understanding of junior high ministry. There are professional youth workers, Susan Hay and Kara Lassen Oliver; volunteer leaders, Jim Bielefeldt and Lynne Wells Graziano; and junior high students, Gabriella Graziano and Liz Bielinski. Their voices add a rich texture to the book that help keep the book grounded in the context of day to day ministry with junior highs.

Jump In!

I'll admit it...I was a mess. I was one of those students that we all shutter to think about. In junior high, I would lie awake at night dreaming of ways to get into mischief at church. On top of that, I was a leader. I could easily get most of the people in the group to follow my example. On one particular retreat, I was at the top of my game. My youth pastor, Dale, had returned to the church to attend a funeral of one of the saints of our congregation. He left us with a few parents and volunteers who were new to junior high ministry and that was the only opening I needed. In a matter of hours, I had led the group in sinking four canoes in the middle of the lake, moving all of the mattresses from the bunks to the roof, and eating all of the food that was supposed to last the weekend.

What I couldn't identify at the time was that I was doing everything I could to make myself unlovable. Because of a difficult family situation coupled with the natural insecurities of being an early adolescent, I had convinced myself that I was unlovable. I was simply trying to prove my theory true. But Dale wouldn't relent. No matter how hard I tried, Dale still loved me. At every turn, even after that infamous retreat, Dale proved his love by accepting me and loving me for who I was. Through his example, I learned what love and grace are all about. Because of his perseverance I opened my heart to Christ and ventured into the journey of discipleship. As a result of his compassion, I developed a passion for junior high ministry.

Behind all of the games and activities, under the details and discipline, and beyond the retreats and lock-ins, there lies in all youth workers a passion for junior high ministry. Each of you has a desire to help early adolescents encounter the life changing, world-shaking—Jesus that has radically altered your life. You want to share the great news of God's unconditional love with young people. That's why you have picked up this book. More importantly, that is why you have signed on for the wild adventure of junior high ministry.

There is no doubt—junior high ministry is a messy business. On top of the food fights, bodily noises, and goofy games, you encounter youth who are making life-shaping decisions about drugs, sex, and faith. This ministry is not for the faint of heart. By ninth grade, most young people have formed the values that will shape their future. Junior high ministry is the church's last, best opportunity to be involved in the process of shaping those values. It is an opportunity to share the good news of God's love with students who are ready and able to be shaped by it. It is an invitation to jump into the middle of the mess and bring a word of hope and grace.

That is why I believe that the calling to junior high ministry is the highest calling in the church. Those of you who have the courage, the fortitude, and the commitment to love and serve junior highs shoulder an incredible burden. In many cases you will never see the results of your labor. Most youth will never tell you how great you are or how much they appreciate you. In fact, most nights you will feel under appreciated and over worked. But take heart. The impact you are having is eternal and the rewards are beyond compare. Take the invitation. Join me in the middle of the mess. It's worth every minute.

High Ideals

Parent and Youth Expectations for Junior High Ministry

by Lynne Wells Graziano, with Gabriella Graziano

As a parent who has volunteered in youth ministry for many years, I was sure that my children would be at every activity once they entered middle school. After all, hadn't I wondered to myself about "what type of parent" would allow their child to miss youth group? God teaches us humility through our children, and I have been learning alongside my seventh grader Gabriella. Her observations, her experiences, and her reasons for not going to youth group hopefully will provide insight for youth pastors and leaders in setting up a junior high ministry.

Continuity counts! We moved to a new area when Gabriella was finishing fifth grade and joined a church before she started sixth grade. The church had a youth minister she liked and a group of fabulous, warm volunteers. In less than six months, the youth minister left suddenly, without a chance to communicate with the youth left behind. Neither of us would want to suggest pastors should stay indefinitely at a church simply for continuity's sake; however, transition times can leave youth with a sense of rejection. While pastoral continuity is preferable, volunteers, church leaders, and the pastoral staff must communicate with youth during times of transition.

Personal communication reflects caring. In the past year and a half, I have seen Gabriella get really excited about going to an event three times. The first time was when she received a phone call invitation from an adult volunteer to a pizza party. The second time was when the leaders of her girls' small group Bible study planned a "girls night out." The third was when one of those same leaders sent her a handwritten, postcard "invitation" to Wednesday night fellowship. As a leader, I have always known personal contact makes a difference, and I've seen that illustrated dramatically in my own home. If your program is so large that you can't call, write, or e-mail everyone occasionally, make sure that you have faithful volunteers who will.

Minimize cliques and boy/girl tensions. Eliminating cliques would be a higher ideal, but short of that we need to work diligently to minimize the opportunity for clique development and gender tension. Junior High is a hormonally charged time, but we shouldn't assume that every boy and girl there wants to stare at and interact with the opposite sex. When appropriate, separate junior highs by gender, allowing them "safe space" to grow and learn.

Help them grow in faith. When asked what she wanted to do at youth group, Gabriella said, "Learn about God." Pretty simple. Yet we fill our schedules with programs, events, lock-ins and activities that often fail to advance our kids' faith. What sets youth group apart from every other activity is Jesus. Of course they want to have fun, often they want to be entertained, but always they want to see Jesus in their leaders, be reminded of what Scripture teaches, and be surrounded by love and acceptance.

Involve them in missions and service. When we moved, we left a church that had junior high summer service projects every year. Gabriella wants to have mission experiences now, in a close to home setting. Seek out ways for the youth in your program to serve locally, in "small" ways and then draw them into a summer program where they can intensively serve others and grow in faith. I've watched a small group of junior high youth serve breakfast to a large group of inner city homeless men: the youth are open, friendly, enthusiastic and at ease at this age. Build up their young servants' hearts before they have a chance to become cynical or hardened to the plight of the less fortunate.

Offer alternatives, when possible. My daughter is athletic, but she doesn't want to prove that at youth group. Inflatable games, sport competitions, and run around activities are great for many, but not all. Make the intellectual, the introverted, and the non-athletic students feel welcomed by planning parallel activities that appeal to their interests. Your recognition that strong differences and divergent opinions exist at this age reinforces the concept of many parts forming the Body of Christ.

Rotate retreats and other big events. For youth who are committed to sports teams or other seasonal activities, try to plan retreats at different times of the year. While fall may be the best time for a retreat, occasionally plan a winter or a spring one. While your "numbers" may not be as high, the impact you can make on the lives of the students who appreciate a retreat that fits their schedule may be priceless.

Faith, hope, and love, these three abide. Youth group and youth events are often where decisions for Christ are made. As a parent, I give thanks for those kinds of opportunities! Encourage the youth in their individual faith journeys, by sharing your own journey and modeling a Christian life. Offer them hope, not just for eternity, but also for the present and the not-so-distant future. Junior high is fraught with struggles; yet you can offer them hope and encouragement in a way parents can't! Be generous in your love of them. Even when they break your rules, your furniture, or your heart—love them unconditionally. Believe it or not, you likely will be remembered as one of their role models, a leader who truly shaped their life for eternity!

Chapter 1
A Theological Framework for Junior High Ministry

Junior High Ministry and Practical Theology

What does the gospel mean to a fourteen-year-old girl whose father is abusive? How can I get rid of cliques in my youth group? Should we have communion at the end of our confirmation retreat? Do I take my junior high students on a mission trip? What kind of games do we play in youth group? All of these questions have one thing in common—they are essentially theological inquiries. How you answer these questions will be informed by your theological understanding of the life of Christ and the life of the church. Whenever you answer one of these questions, you are doing theology whether you know it or not. This is practical theology.

Starting Right defines practical theology as "reflection about how God works in Christian action, in order to set forth norms and strategies for practices that faithfully participate in God's transformation of the church and the world" (*Starting Right*, 29). Practical theology is allowing what we know about God to shape what we do in ministry. Too often in youth ministry, the reverse is true. We allow our ministries and programs to shape what we know and teach about God.

> *Practical theology is allowing what we know about God to shape what we do in ministry.*

Developing a theology of junior high ministry begins with laying claim to the essentials of your personal theology and those of your tradition. What are those elements of faith that are essential to your understanding of God? Who are youth in relation to God? In the following pages of this chapter, I want to express a theology of junior high ministry. This is born out of my United Methodist tradition, my personal experience of God, my understanding of the Scripture, and my knowledge of junior high youth. This is in no way an exhaustive theology of ministry and chances are you may disagree with me at various points. That's great! I hope that this chapter will challenge you to look at your own theological touchstones and push you to develop a practical theology for your ministry with junior high youth.

Understanding God

During college a good friend challenged me to define my theology. John was not a Christian and he loved to provoke discussions that would force me to think deeply about the surface convictions that I held from my Christian upbringing. He would often ask me the same question: "Can you summarize your faith in one word?" Inevitably we would reach a point in the discussion where I was annoyed because he wouldn't accept any of my answers, and he was deeply satisfied because I couldn't give a good answer. After graduation, I became a youth pastor in a United Methodist church. Almost five years later, I called John and left a message on his answering machine. "John, this is Drew. I have one word for you—grace." And I hung up the phone. Two weeks later, John called me and we went to lunch to discuss my answer. It seems that in the maze of practicing ministry I found the word that shaped who I was and what I understood about God.

In the Wesleyan tradition, grace is understood in many ways. Essentially, grace is God's activity in the lives of humans through the person of Jesus Christ. Grace expresses the very heart and character of God. God is love. God's desire is for all of humankind to know and experience that love. Through the gift of grace in the person of Jesus Christ, God makes that love known to humanity. In *Amazing Grace*, Kathleen Norris says: "God will find a way to let us know that [God] is with us in this place, wherever we are, however far we think we've run." (Riverhead Books, 151). We can do nothing to earn it. We can do nothing to deserve it. It is just there—wherever you are—calling you to respond. That is grace. That is the message of the Christian gospel. That is my foundation for junior high ministry, not that I make sure that every junior higher verbalizes the meaning of grace, but that through the church's ministry every junior high student experiences grace.

Prevenient Grace

God's gift of grace is expressed through various ways in human activity. Prevenient grace refers to God's presence in the lives of all people before they are even aware of it. Prevenient grace is the work of the Holy Spirit to gently (or sometimes not so gently) nudge people toward an awareness of God's presence and their need for deliverance from sin. This truth is essential for junior high ministry. Many of the young people that pass through the doors of your church have no idea that God is present in their lives. In fact, many times you might not be able to recognize God's presence in their lives. But prevenient grace calls us to see God in the eyes of each young person—the rebel, the leader, the agitator, the rude, the awkward. And prevenient grace reminds us of one essential truth of junior high ministry—never give up!

Mark came to our church as an awkward, lonely young man from an unstable family. He was often rude and obnoxious. He rarely paid attention to anything that was going on in youth group and often became a disruption for the rest of the youth. More than that, he scared me. There was a look in his eyes that conveyed his disdain for anything and everything about the church. For several months, I tried to minister to Mark. I called his home, I sent him notes and e-mails, and I talked to him in the halls every Sunday. But, that is where I stopped. After several months, my relationship with Mark deteriorated to the bare minimum. Within a year, Mark was gone from the congregation. To be honest, I didn't think about Mark until I was preparing a sermon on prevenient grace. Convicted by my own failure, I attempted to reach out to Mark but continued to get ignored. After that, I added Mark to my regular prayer list and committed myself to looking for the presence of God in each and every student I encountered. A few months ago, I saw Mark in the mall. He's doing great. He has joined another church and is an active part of their ministry. As we said goodbye, I held out my hand and simply said, "I'm sorry." He smiled and turned away. In his eyes at that moment, I could clearly see what I wasn't able to before. I thank God for that youth leader who was able to see past Mark's masks and minister to a hurting young man.

Junior high youth need to know that they are loved despite their perceived faults, failings, and foibles. They need to know about Jesus Christ and his love for them. They need to be assured, over and over again, that God is with them.

One of the works of prevenient grace, as defined by John Wesley, is convincing grace. Convincing grace is the work of God that moves people to recognize their need for God's forgiveness. Sharing the gospel story with junior high students involves sharing honestly about the human condition. Because sin is a part of who we are, we stand in need of forgiveness. A healthy understanding of grace does not avoid our radical need for forgiveness. However, we must avoid a picture of grace that puts us on one side of a great chasm totally separated from God's love by sin—nothing can separate us from the love of God (Romans 8:39). Prevenient grace tells us that God is with us even in our sin. John Wesley, in his sermon "On Working Out Our Own Salvation" says, "No man is wholly void of the grace of God." Convincing grace moves us to a "yes" to God's redeeming work in our lives. Effective junior high ministry always sees the glimpse of God's love present in each student and encourages students to act on God's presence in their lives.

At all costs, we must avoid using guilt or fear as a tactic for presenting the gospel. Early adolescents are motivated by a desire to please adults and peers. They are likely to respond in fear if they believe that we will be disappointed in them or think less of them. Convincing grace is fundamentally the work of God to bring people to an awareness of their need for forgiveness. It is not the work of youth leaders, parents, or pastors. Our role is to present the gospel faithfully, pointing to the love of God, the death and resurrection of Jesus Christ, and the call to follow.

For the first several years of my ministry, I was burdened by the overwhelming feeling that I had to save the world—or at least all of the kids in my youth group and the surrounding community. I was trained in college to help "bring kids to a point of decision" about faith and salvation. Unfortunately, I took this to mean that it was my job to convince them of their need for the saving grace of God. Understanding convincing grace as wholly God's work, not ours, frees us from assuming the responsibility of "saving souls" and leads us to a ministry that works hard to place youth "in the way of grace."

Justifying Grace

Prevenient grace nudges us into awareness of God's presence in our lives. Convincing grace brings us to an understanding of our need for divine forgiveness. Through justifying grace, God reaches out to the repentant sinner with accepting and forgiving grace. The Holy Spirit is at work in justification to enact a real change in the human heart. Justification is the act of God by which we are forgiven of our sin and restored into a right relationship with God through faith in Jesus Christ.

Junior high youth may not fully understand the ultimate consequences of their decision to choose Jesus; but that does not mean that they should not be given the opportunity to make a decision to accept the gift of salvation through Jesus Christ. Rather, they need to be presented with opportunities to make decisions for Christ over and over again. They need to understand that these decisions come every time they make choices about how to talk to their parents, how to treat their peers, and how to respond to their teachers. Junior high ministry needs to be less about dramatic conversion experiences and more about a constantly unfolding understanding of the life of faith.

Sanctifying Grace

Sanctification is the work of the Holy Spirit in the life of the Christian that leads to an increased understanding of divine love and the practice of human love. Sanctifying grace empowers believers to live out their faith as they become more Christlike in word and actions. Sanctifying grace is at work in junior high students when they allow themselves to be used to reach out to others with the love of God. At their core, junior high students need to feel needed. They want to know that their lives make a difference and their actions can make a difference in someone else's life.

Throughout our ministry with junior high students we will catch glimpses of God's sanctifying grace at work in the lives of young people. John was a young man who provided some of my greatest moments of frustration in ministry, and some of my most treasured memories. He often caused trouble, seldom listened, and hardly ever followed directions. Yet, John was incredibly attuned to the work of God in his life. While serving on a mission trip in Washington D.C., John reached out in love and became a godbearer to complete strangers—and to me. One day, while we were discussing the issue of homelessness, John wandered away from the group. Before I noticed, he was on the bench sitting next to someone that I was obviously uncomfortable with. As I approached to pull John back to the group, he introduced me to his friend. "Drew, this is Ernie. He's been telling me what its like to live on the streets in the most powerful city in the world. He wants to help us this afternoon at the food pantry." While I was with a group discussing homelessness, John was listening to a homeless man tell his story. He forced me to think about justice, empowerment, and transformation—and he was "only" twelve years old. That is the awesome power of sanctifying grace at work in the life of a junior higher.

Grace, embodied in Jesus Christ, is the lens through which I understand God and the mold that shapes my practice of ministry. It is a gift, offered freely to all people—including junior high youth. Grace calls me to see God in the eyes of every young person I encounter. Grace, in all its forms, insists that I never give up on a difficult student. Grace demands that I share honestly with students our need for divine forgiveness. Grace pushes me to regularly offer opportunities for young

> *Grace calls me to see God in the eyes of every young person I encounter.*

people to make decisions to follow Christ. Grace charges me to provide openings for students to allow God to work in and through them, empowering them to become more like Christ.

Understanding Junior High Youth

Developing a practical theology for junior high ministry also involves understanding who junior high students are in relation to God. Junior high youth have a special place in the kingdom of God and an essential role in the Body of Christ. Junior high ministry affirms early adolescents for who they are in the eyes of God and offers them glimpses of who they can be through the power of the Holy Spirit.

First, junior high youth must be affirmed as children of God, created in God's image. Many early adolescents doubt their self-worth and struggle with their self-image. They define themselves in terms of how they believe others see them.

They look in the mirror and often do not like what they see. They see other students whisper and automatically feel that they are the object of their ridicule. They flip through the pages of teen magazines and become convinced that they cannot measure up to the world's standards. In our ministries, early adolescents need to be convinced that they are God's masterpiece, created in the image and likeness of God. "For we are God's workmanship, created in Christ Jesus to do good works, which God prepared in advance for us to do" (Ephesians 2:10, NIV). What we do in ministry, not just what we say, needs to convey to young people that they are special and gifted.

Second, early adolescents need to know that they are accepted for who they are and loved unconditionally. Unmistakably, the church is called to let junior high youth know that God receives them just as they are—that God loves them regardless of what they do or don't do. They do not need to accomplish anything, to achieve anything, or to earn anything. Too often, young people find it difficult to live up to the standards set by their peers, their schools, and unfortunately, their churches. "In a world that seems to measure, compare, and rank you from the moment you are born, the good news is that you belong to God and are loved by God, and there is nothing you can do to remove yourself from God's love" (*Starting Right*, 249). In the church, early adolescents need to encounter this unconditional love and be freed from the competitive nature of every other area of their lives.

> *In our ministries, early adolescents need to be convinced that they are God's masterpiece, created in the image and likeness of God.*

Finally, the church must affirm that junior high students are essential to the church's life and God's mission in the world. Like any other part of the Body of Christ, junior high students are irreplaceable. To paraphrase the apostle Paul, the elders of the church cannot say to junior high students, "because you are not old, you do not belong to the body" any more than a junior higher can say to an elder, "because you have been around too long, we have voted you off of the island." The often crazy, dysfunctional entity known as the church is a gathering place for all of God's children—young and old, rich and poor. Rather than being sent to the youth room in the basement for games and pizza, junior high youth need to be embraced by the entire community, nurtured in the faith and included in the mission of the church. Junior high youth are the Body of Christ. They are the church of today as well as the church of tomorrow! "God has combined the members of the body and has given greater honor to the parts that lacked it, so that there should be no division in the body, but that its parts should have equal concern for each other" (1 Corinthians 12:24b-25).

Theology of Junior High Ministry in Practice

Flowing from theological convictions, essential practices of junior high ministry emerge. These practices form the backbone of a comprehensive understanding of junior high youth ministry. These are not program components to be read like ingredients in a recipe. Rather, they are practices of faith that flow from my theological convictions and give shape to my understanding of junior high ministry. These practices, essentially, are the same as that of a healthy church. Junior high youth do not need a watered-down faith. They need to experience the grace of God and the practices of faith in ways that are developmentally appropriate.

Community: God intends for the life of faith to be lived in the context of community. The development of the earliest church in the book of Acts and the writings of the apostle Paul underscore the fact that the Christian faith is not a matter of privatized religion. Similarly, one of the greatest developmental needs of junior high youth is having a sense of belonging—to be in communion with others. Younger youth need to feel that they are an integral part of a group of like-minded peers. In a group, junior high students are looking to be accepted, to be loved, and to be safe. At its best, the church of Jesus Christ is an ideal place to meet this need.

Worship: In worship, the community of faith gathers in the presence of God to offer praise and thanksgiving, to be shaped by the living Word of God, to be filled with the Holy Spirit, and sent to live in the world as disciples of Jesus Christ. Worship moves us outside of our comfort zones into a living encounter with the Holy. Junior high youth are desperately seeking a God that they can see, feel, and touch. Worship with junior highs does not happen only for an hour on Sunday mornings. It happens every time you provide an opportunity for youth to enter into God's presence and be renewed and transformed.

Catechesis: Catechesis is simply the act of passing on the faith through teaching and instruction, sometimes through question and answer memorization. Some churches use a confirmation program that passes on the faith to younger youth and invites them to participate in the ritual of confirming their baptism and claiming the Christian faith for themselves. This process is not about the information that we give junior highs, but the life in which we invite them to participate. When we pass on the faith we are not transmitting an endless series of facts and lessons, but a way of living in the world as disciples of Jesus Christ.

Mercy and Justice: Hand in hand, these practices of the faith spring from an understanding of the sanctifying grace of God working to make us more like Christ. As God works in the lives of junior highs, we must provide opportunities for them to be agents of God's mercy and justice in the world around them. Service projects, mission trips, and social justice advocacy are all ways that junior highs can participate in the work of Christ in the world.

Play: Play is a spiritual practice that underscores my theology of junior high ministry. The very nature of God is playful and life giving. God wants us to laugh, to occasionally be free from our burdens, and to enjoy being in God's presence. Younger youth need to have a place where they can put aside their concerns, play using their bodies and imaginations, and bask in the love and grace of God.

Your theology of junior high ministry will be the basis of your ministry. If your theology of junior high ministry is to keep them occupied half of the time and fill them up with memory verses for the other half, then your group will probably not evolve into a committed group of fully-devoted followers of Jesus Christ. If you are in constant prayer for your group, see the face of God in each one of your students, and long for Christ to be formed in them as you journey the road of faith together, then you will most likely see your group grow and thrive in faith. Don't take developing a theology for youth ministry lightly, but make it an immediate priority and use that theology as a foundation and framework for your ministry—whether you're just starting out, or you've been in ministry for years.

Junior High Ministry

Chapter 2

A Primer on Junior High Development

Elizabeth looked in the mirror after trying on her third dress. Each of them, she thought, made her look bigger than she really was. She wrestled with anxiety, depression, and poor self worth. "Why are they making me go to this stupid dance anyway," she asked herself? "Everyone will just make fun of me, and I will be miserable all night." She finally settled on an outfit, went out the door to the dance, and came back after having "the best night of her life."

Across town, Jane prepared for the dance quickly. "Mom, I've got to hurry up. I'm in charge and I need to be there an hour before anyone else." All month Jane had been busily preparing for the annual fall dance. As student council president she was responsible for all of the school's social activities. In addition, Jane is president of her junior high youth group and co-chair of the math club. Amazingly, she also finds time to volunteer at her grandmother's nursing home and swim for the YWCA.

Arturo has been looking forward to the dance for weeks. He had finally mustered up the courage to ask Elizabeth to dance. Of course, he didn't know how to dance, but he knew how he felt every time he was around her. He also knew that everyone would make fun of him because he was so short and she wasn't. It all came down to one question—which meant more to him, her or his friends?

Ethan sat on the couch playing video games. He had no interest in going and he certainly didn't want to dance. He invited Sarah and Marcus over for the night to hang out and play games. The three had been best friends since kindergarten and were commonly referred to as the three musketeers. Now, alone on the couch, Ethan felt dejected because Marcus and Sarah were both going to the dance—together! They started "going out" a month ago, and Ethan has been on the outside looking in ever since.

Each of these young people shares one thing in common—they are all twelve years old. Their physical, emotional, and intellectual maturity vary greatly, but they are all early adolescents. Elizabeth worries about her physical appearance because she has developed much quicker than everyone else in her class. Arturo struggles because he feels that he hasn't developed at all. He is emotionally ready to think about relationships with the opposite sex, but he hasn't physically grown a bit. Ethan worries because his friends are already dating and he wants to play games and have a sleepover. Jane, on the other hand, is already taking on various leadership roles in her school and church. It's hard to believe that they are all the same age.

Adults who have the task of working with early adolescents face great challenges and great rewards. Developmentally, junior high students are beginning to explore who they are and develop their identity. They are learning to think abstractly and wrestle with issues of faith and life. They are testing their values and trying on different roles within their family and peer groups. At the same time, their bodies are developing rapidly and with that comes a whole new set of issues—sexual identity, relationships with the opposite sex, self-image, among a host of other issues. Junior highs can be frustratingly unstable, exhaustingly energetic, and maddeningly conflicted. Yet, at the same time, they are at a point when their values are being shaped, their concept of self is being molded, and their identity is being developed. There is simply no greater time to be in ministry with adolescents than the junior high years.

One thing is certain: a "typical" or "average" junior high student does not exist. Each adolescent moves through the developmental process at a different pace. Some young people will be advanced physically while developing slower emotionally. Some will advance cognitively while socially they are behind most of their peers. It is important that you understand the different factors of emotional, moral, cognitive, social, and physical development. More important, however, is that you take the time to know the individuals in your youth group. What are the individual's developmental needs? What risks is she likely to face? What is his family situation? The most important thing about junior high ministry is developing relationships with each student and finding ways to support them as they go about the task of identity formation.

Your role and the role of the faith community are crucial to the developmental process. The church has a unique voice in critical areas facing early adolescents.

> *When early adolescents struggle with bodily self-image and sexual identity, the church can affirm that they are created by God, and they are good.*

The theology of vocation tells us that each young person is born with a purpose, a mission, in the kingdom of God. Early adolescence is a great time to instill self-worth and an understanding that each young person has been created and gifted by God. Scripture also claims that we are all born in the image and likeness of God, a masterpiece of the Creator. When early adolescents struggle with bodily self-image and sexual identity, the church can affirm that they are created by God, and they are good. As young people make decisions about values that will shape their lives, the church can speak with a clear voice about justice, service, and compassion.

This chapter will provide an overview of early adolescent development — physically, intellectually, socially, morally, and emotionally. In doing so, we will draw implications for the task of youth ministry. Remember, these are generalities not meant to categorize any individual student, but to inform your understanding of the developmental process.

Physical Development

I will never forget my first gym class in junior high when I discovered that I would actually have to change clothes in a room full of my peers. The anxiety quickly turned into an illness as I tried to avoid going to gym class on the first day. I ran to the nurse's office and asked to call my mom. Noticing my fear, the nurse asked me what class I had next. "Gym," I said calmly, "but that's not why I'm sick!" The kind nurse allowed me to change in her office and sent me back to gym class. On my way out, she called me to a corner of her office and said, "if you are ever afraid again, just remember that everyone is in the same boat as you."

Of course, to a twelve-year-old boy, her statement was ridiculous. Did she know that John had hair in his armpits, or that Max had already kissed two girls? However, the kindhearted nurse was not saying that we were all the same, but that we were all dealing with the same thing—rapidly changing bodies—and that we were all afraid of what was happening.

These changes, beginning with the onset of puberty that generally occurs between the ages of nine and fifteen (age eleven for most adolescents), are traumatizing for many young people. In the first place, early adolescents are experiencing rapid and irregular physical growth that often causes awkward uncoordinated movements. Sports can be particularly humiliating for young people who are working so hard at impressing their friends. In addition, secondary sex characteristics begin to appear along with an increased sexual awareness. These changes typically occur more quickly in girls, often causing great difficulties for friends of the same age. Many young people become self-conscious when they exhibit physical changes more rapidly or more slowly than their peers. There is often great comparison between individuals and the "idealized other." In addition, what is commonly referred to as an abundance of energy characteristic of junior highs is caused by significant hormonal changes that also cause restlessness and fatigue.

These rapid changes and the constant anxiety that accompany them bring several dangers to the surface. Alcoholism and drug abuse among early adolescents have increased significantly. It is not unusual for young people who question their own worth because of poor self-image to turn to illegal substances that can ease the pain of isolation and rejection. In addition, suicide and depression among early adolescents cause significant challenges for junior high ministry. School violence, domestic violence, and increased sexual activity are also areas of great concern.

> *Young people need to know that their lives bear the fingerprints of the Creator and that their lives have value.*

Several implications for junior high ministry stem from an understanding of the physical development of early adolescents. In the first place, young people need to hear again and again their position as individuals of sacred worth. They need to know that their lives bear the fingerprints of the Creator and that their lives have value. Young people also need help accepting themselves for who they have been created to be. In an age when junior highs turn on the television or read a magazine and compare themselves with perfect figures, beautiful faces, and expansive muscles, they need to accept their bodies and appreciate their own inner, and outer, beauty.

In addition, leaders in junior high ministry must not be afraid to tackle issues of sexual identity, sexual intercourse, and relationships with the opposite sex. Churches need to affirm all youth for the sexual beings that they were created to be. We must provide a comfortable, nonthreatening environment where young people can talk freely about the changes that are happening to their bodies and the feelings that accompany these changes. Young people must be able to explore their attitudes about relationships and intercourse in a supportive environment with adults and peers that they trust and who encourage acceptance. The church must also speak with a clear voice about God's design for sexual intercourse; the injustice of sexual inequality and gender stereotypes, the dangers of sexually transmitted diseases, and the problem of sexual violence.

Emotional Development

JOHN: *"Mom, I don't think I'm going to church anymore. It's boring and everyone there is a hypocrite."*

MOM: *"You better believe you are going to go to church. Now you march yourself right upstairs and get dressed."*

JOHN: *"But mom..."*

MOM: *"Don't "but mom" me, get dressed!*

(In the car)

JOHN: *"Mom, I really don't think making me go will make any difference. I don't even believe in God so why should I go to church?"*

MOM: *(Starting to cry) "Because we go to church. That's what we do. Now you will go with a smile on your face and you will like it!"*

Have you ever had anyone like John in your ministry? What's more, have you ever had some parents come to you crying and questioning why their son or daughter doesn't believe in the things that they hold most sacred? The mother and son in this fictional dialogue are not unique. In fact, they represent a good portion of early adolescents and their parents who struggle through the adolescent emotional development.

The emotional development of early adolescents is often the area most difficult to understand and the one that causes the greatest trouble for adults who work with junior highs. Junior highs at this stage begin to move away from parental influence and exert their own independence. This often includes a seeming rejection of family and moral values that causes heartache for many parents and youth workers. This is a crucial part of early adolescent development and not simply the behavior of a rebellious teenager. In order to take the values that they have been taught into adulthood, younger youth must be allowed to let go of them and re-claim them for themselves. If parents and the church respond with disbelief and anger, the young people will see that as a rejection of them and will likely close the door on these treasured values. If they encounter grace and openness to exploration and questioning, they are likely to continue their search for identity within the context of the family and faith community.

Other characteristics of early adolescent emotional development are: frequently fluctuating between emotional peaks of excitement and depths of moodiness, developing interest in ethics and morality while forming individual opinions, developing decision-making skills, having low self-esteem, having a high level of self-consciousness, and being self absorbed.

These characteristics make junior high ministry so frustrating at times and so wonderfully invigorating at others. Who among us has not had a young person commit their lives to Christ at 9:30 and give another student a "swirly" by 10:00? To do junior high ministry without burning out and giving up, we have to understand that this is normal behavior appropriate to their emotional development. That doesn't mean that we don't correct poor behavioral choices, but we do need to understand why junior highs make some of the decisions that they do.

The first implication of emotional development for junior high youth ministry is the need to create a safe, nurturing environment. Every young person who walks into your group is wondering whether or not he or she is important to you and to the church. Remembering names, extending smiles and appropriate physical touch, and providing a nonthreatening space for growth and exploration are all important in junior high ministry. Junior highs need to feel loved, safe, and secure. Second, we must be careful to avoid any activities that will cause embarrassment or increase self-consciousness. Activities such as competitive sports and practical jokes can lead to increasing anxiety and an unwillingness to participate. If a junior high student feels that they he might be picked on, laughed at, or made an example of, he may not return to your group.

Another implication for junior high ministry is the need to focus on serving others and working for justice. As junior highs struggle between being self-absorbed and wanting to be needed by others, the church has an opportunity to shape their thinking beyond themselves. By providing opportunities for young people to serve others, you are increasing their own self-worth while also stressing the importance of caring for the needs of others. In addition, as younger youth begin to grapple with issues of justice and fairness, the church can help foster their desire to stand up for the concerns of others. Many junior high students have worked against child-labor practices in Third World countries, campaigned against tobacco companies that target their peers, and stood against unfair treatment of the homeless in their communities. You need to promote a need for both service and justice as junior highs begin to define and understand their moral convictions.

> *As junior highs struggle between being self-absorbed and wanting to be needed by others, the church has an opportunity to shape their thinking beyond themselves.*

Intellectual Development

My three-year-old son has been driving me crazy lately. Every day, beginning with the first words out of his mouth, he asks a million questions about our family, the earth, God, and anything else you can imagine. Why do birds fly? Why did you and mommy get married? Why do we go to church? Why did Aunt Irene die? Why does Jesus love me? Worse yet, he won't listen to my answers! Inevitably I will answer the same question nine times and he will follow with the same response: why? Of course, this is not because he does not respect his father or disagrees with my answers, but because he is simply developing his ability to ask questions. In junior high, young people begin to ask themselves many of the same questions but they are also able to begin grappling with answers.

Early adolescents are beginning to advance in three specific arenas of thought:

- They are beginning to think **abstractly**. For instance, junior high youth can begin to think of the church as being more than the building that they walk into on Sunday morning. Instead, they can wrestle with the church as a community of Christians and as an extension of God's presence in the world.

- They are developing the ability to think **hypothetically**. While children focus on actual, predictable elements of a situation, adolescents begin to imagine what is possible and the different possibilities for solving a problem.

- They are beginning to think **logically**. As their thinking becomes more abstract, adolescents begin to test their thinking against different ideas to establish their understanding of truth (*Adolescence*, 179).

One of the most difficult challenges facing junior high ministries is developing creative ways to teach biblical and theological truths to developing minds. Active and practical learning experiences for early adolescents are essential. Junior highs need educational experiences that can show a direct correlation to their daily lives and the issues with which they concern themselves. Learning experiences must also provide a high level of interaction and the ability for young people to create or discover meaning. Further, early adolescents need to be able to test their thinking against that of their peers in a nonthreatening environment. Small-group experiences where they can test ideas, wrestle with abstract thoughts, and create solutions to problems appeal to junior high youth.

Another important aspect of creative teaching is finding ways to teach young people who learn using different forms of intelligence. Howard Gardner argues for seven forms of intelligence: musical, bodily-kinesthetic, logical-mathematical, linguistic, spatial, interpersonal (understanding others), and intrapersonal (understanding self) (*Adolescence*, 167–169). Unfortunately, many of our teaching-learning opportunities in junior high ministry focus on the linguistic (words and language) and the interpersonal. In addition to these intelligences, young people need opportunities to learn through music, through introspection, and through motion and dance. Find an active-learning based curriculum, such as *Faith in Motion* from Abingdon Press, that can help you develop lessons that teach to different intelligences.

At this stage of intellectual development, early adolescents feel a great need to show competence and gain further achievement. Because the gap between good and poor students widens, early adolescents often struggle with feelings of inadequacy. Young people can begin to feel as if they are not as smart as their peers, which can lead to frustration or even helplessness.

In ministering with junior high students, provide plenty of opportunities for them to succeed—not in competition with their peers, but through collaboration and teamwork. Junior highs need to be encouraged to think together about problems and work together to apply solutions. Each year I challenge the members of the confirmation class to develop service projects that they can perform with their mentors. I encourage them to work in teams with other classmates and their mentors to identify a need, develop a way to meet that need, and carry out their solution. Toward the end of the year we have a service fair for the entire church. The confirmation students set up displays of their completed projects and provide information for other members of the congregation to be involved in their ministry. This fair not only highlights the students' ministry, but also gets the entire congregation involved in service and mission. At the same time, the confirmands show pride in their accomplishments and develop a strong sense of achievement.

Social Development

Christmas of my seventh grade year was nearing. I pleaded with my mom to take me to the mall where I spent two hours buying gifts for all of my friends in school. I bought posters, tapes, and a stuffed animal for the girl I was "going with." When I got in the car and my mother saw all of the bags, she asked, "Show me what you got your brothers." I froze. I could try and lie and say that I got my brother a stuffed animal, or I could tell the truth. After trying the lie and getting "the look," I confessed: "All of the gifts are for my friends." Disappointed, my mom asked, "Well, how much money do you have left?" "About two dollars," I replied, not knowing how much I would upset her. "I just don't understand you. You spend all of your money on your friends and don't seem to care about your own brothers."

While this conversation doesn't happen in every household, it does underscore one of the most significant aspects of early adolescent social development—the increasing role of peer approval. It is easy to see why most parents are frustrated when junior highs begin making decisions based on acceptance by their peers. Was my behavior that Christmas insensitive to my family's needs? Probably. Was it uncharacteristic of early adolescents who are struggling to gain acceptance and belonging among their peers? Not at all. Parents and youth leaders need to understand that a young person who seeks peer approval and acceptance is not rejecting family or religious values but is making a statement of independence and taking a necessary step in the developmental process. Parents and youth leaders can help in this process by supporting an adolescent's attempts to gain the respect of peers in healthy ways and pointing out some of the dangers inherent in trying to fit in.

Later in the evening of my shopping trip, my mother came into my room and sat on the end of my bed. "I think it is great that you bought gifts for your friends at school. I know that they are really important to you and that you want them to know how much you care about them. I also know that you care about your brothers and you will want to show them that, too." She went on to give me an opportunity to "earn" twenty more dollars to shop for my brothers. For the next two years, she supported my involvement and interaction with my friends while also finding ways to reassert our family values in a nonjudgmental way.

In junior high youth ministry, you must provide an atmosphere where young people feel like they fit in and have acceptance among their peers. Cliques are not always a bad thing in junior high youth ministry. Young people are developing networks of friends that they can both relate to and develop trusting relationships with as they wrestle with the stresses of growing up. At the same time, cliques are harmful when they exclude, ridicule, or isolate other youth. The youth ministry needs to be a place where every young person is accepted and finds a place to belong. I choose to involve high school students in the junior high ministry because they can easily identify the young people who may be considered "uncool" by others in the group. Because of the esteem that they command, senior highs can raise the acceptance level of those students.

Another significant aspect of early adolescent social development is the cementing of sex roles. In a society where young people are inundated with music, movies, magazines, and television shows that define sex and relationships as being based on physical appearance and animalistic attraction, young people struggle with understanding their own sexuality as a gift from God. When "real men" all have tall, athletic bodies and never show emotion, adolescent boys have a hard time measuring up. When young women see twelve-year-old models and singers with "perfect" bodies, they struggle to appreciate their own self-worth. Healthy relationships between adolescents and both members of the opposite sex and members of the same sex help adolescents think through sexuality and arrive at a positive self-concept. The church can provide numerous opportunities for young men and women to interact with one another in positive ways so that they can develop a healthy sense of self in a safe and affirming environment.

The "Jobs" of Early Adolescents

Each stage of life has "jobs" or tasks that every individual needs to learn in order to go on and live a healthy and productive life. Many people who study human development believe that if the jobs at a particular stage are not learned, people get stuck at this stage of development and will be less successful (at work, at home, and within themselves) than those who master these tasks. Early adolescents are at a time of great growth and change equaled only by the ages between one and three. As a result of all of these changes, several important tasks of early adolescents need to be mastered.

This group:

- Becomes aware of rapid physical changes and increases positive feelings about their changing bodies.
- Organizes knowledge and concepts into problem-solving strategies and develops decision-making skills.

- Increases the positive feelings about themselves as they learn new social and sexual roles.
- Becomes increasingly independent.
- Develops friendships with others of both sexes and increases interpersonal communication skills.
- Develops a sense of ownership over their understanding of morality and values.

Educators, parents, and youth workers can ensure that their practices aid in the healthy development of early adolescents. Providing a nurturing and caring environment is key to meeting the needs of young adolescents. As they struggle to develop a positive self-image, an understanding of their sexuality, and healthy relationships with members of the opposite sex, they need to be surrounded by unconditional love and acceptance. While they push against the values and morals that they have grown up with and attempt to define their own ideals, they need to be surrounded by a community that accepts their struggles and questions while providing tools for them to understand Christian principles and practices.

Every developing adolescent needs a trusting relationship with at least one caring adult. Although peers are the primary focus of early adolescents, adolescents desperately need adults in their lives who will listen to their concerns, share in their struggles, model healthy relationships, and embody the love of Jesus Christ. There are several approaches to fostering relationships between adults and early adolescents. One concept that has worked is assigning adult mentors to journey with young people throughout a year of confirmation or three years of junior high. Other churches have asked different groups of adults to work with individuals and groups of young people.

I cannot stress enough the importance of recognizing the developmental needs of junior highs. Too often we joke about this awkward stage, or focus on just surviving the few years called junior high instead of nurturing, affirming, and celebrating where these unique and gifted youth are in their developmental cycle. Sure, their awkwardness can be funny, and sometimes it may seem like you're just holding on for dear life. But before you innocently belittle a junior higher or schedule only fun nights for junior high ministry, remember that early teens are sacred children of God who have specific needs for affirmation and spiritual growth. Take seriously your call to work with them and meet them where they are to deliver the good news of God's love for each one of them.

Younger Adolescents and Brain Research

by Susan Hay

I love the cartoon strip "ZITS." In one "ZITS" strip, the main character's mom unlatches the top of his head, looks in, and exclaims, "Yes, there is a brain in there!" Teens do have a brain, but it is far from being able to function as an adult brain. Teens are a work in progress.

Neuroscientists now know that the brain, like physical development, develops along its own timetable and is different with each young person. What has recently been confirmed is that the part of the brain that helps determine judgment is the last part of the brain to mature, usually in the early twenties. Therefore, those of us who work with early teens have a unique opportunity to help them exercise their brains. We can help them learn how to understand the world around them, relate to other people and peers, explore abstract ideas, and establish specific moral behaviors. These truly are the wonder years.

As childhood provided lots of opportunities for discovering the physical world around them; the teen years provide lots of opportunities for wondering and pondering. This is the time of possibilities. Many early teens begin thinking "what if?" The question "what if" moves the early teen into being able to think in terms of imagined possibilities. This is an age for idealism. Many see the world through rosy eyes, envisioning an ideal church, school, family, and society. It is also a time when they can drive us nuts by pointing out inconsistencies and exceptions. As in the preschool years, fairness is extremely important.

As you have probably experienced, adolescence is a time of tremendous emotional upheaval—loving a person one minute and hating that same person two minutes later. Some early teens experience wide mood swings that even they do not understand or have control over. The limbic system, where raw emotions are generated, reaches a stage of development in the brain where it moves into overdrive. At the same time the prefrontal cortex, referred to as the seat of civilization, is pretty much asleep at the wheel.

Starting at about age eleven, the brain's frontal lobes begin generating an abundance of new connections (neurons). Neuroscientists have likened this time to a tree growing new roots, twigs, and branches. Some even see this development as a second wave of nerve cell production and elimination similar to the first eighteen months of life. This is the time when young teens will help determine which nerve cells are kept and which are eliminated through the choices they make. Research tells us that youth who are physically active, who read, engage in music by either singing or playing an instrument are better able to increase the quality of their brain functions than those who just hang out or stay obsessed with television. Teens, by the activities they participant in, are choosing what their brains will be good at.

We can play a vital part in helping to create positive activities for early teens to pursue that will have the potential of increasing their brain's capacity for making positive decisions through the activities and programs in which we invite early teens to participate. Helping this age to learn right from wrong, teaching them to take responsibility for their actions, providing healthy interactions with friends, and helping to increase their thinking skills should be just as central in our youth ministry programs as training them for discipleship.

Those of us to who work with early teens need to be aware that this pruning of cells in the early teens brains is something to celebrate as this pruning will actually help the brain become more efficient. Only after the frontal cortex, especially the prefrontal lobes closest to the forehead, has been pruned will teens have the ability to make sound judgments. This "hard-wiring" as neuroscientists call it is also another reason that teens need to be discouraged from experimenting with drugs and alcohol. These activities do have the serious potential of permanently altering the delicate balance of chemicals in their brains. Once again we must be willing to be patient with younger youth since they are not only learning how to live in a new body, but also learning a new way of thinking and acting.

Brain research is also supporting what many of us have known all along— the learning styles of boys and girls are different. Boys have a tendency to be more spatial and need much more physical room in which to work. When boys come in with a load of books, they get spread all over the table, not just in front of them. They need space in which to operate. Being spatial also helps them learn math more easily. Whereas girls have a tendency to not need as much space. They are comfortable sitting in intimate circles and benefit from interaction. Boys tend to be object-oriented. I had a young neighbor once whose main task in life was taking engines apart and putting them back together. He was intrigued for hours with the intricacy of the activity. Girls, on the other hand, tend to be people-oriented; they enjoy conversation. Brain research validates that in situations where early teens can experience challenges and tangible accomplishments, their brain cells are stimulated in a positive and efficient way.

As a part of his doctoral research at Harvard University, Howard Gardner developed a theory of multiple intelligences. In his studies, he discovered that cognitive learning takes many different forms in the brain. Gardner isolated seven different intelligences, or ways people learn. He realized that each individual's brain has a preference on how it acquires and stores information. In order to meet the learning needs of those individuals, you must use a variety of teaching techniques.

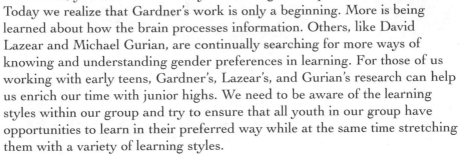

Today we realize that Gardner's work is only a beginning. More is being learned about how the brain processes information. Others, like David Lazear and Michael Gurian, are continually searching for more ways of knowing and understanding gender preferences in learning. For those of us working with early teens, Gardner's, Lazear's, and Gurian's research can help us enrich our time with junior highs. We need to be aware of the learning styles within our group and try to ensure that all youth in our group have opportunities to learn in their preferred way while at the same time stretching them with a variety of learning styles.

Last, neuroscientists express concern about the sleep deprivation of teens. As mentioned before, early adolescence is a time of rapid growth both physically and in the brain. A lot is going on with the early teen that requires tremendous energy just to keep their heads above water. Many teens are up before the crack of dawn to catch school buses and then don't get to bed until late at night. As adults who work with early teens we need to be aware of the need for appropriate rest. Scientists say that youth in this age group need a minimum of eight hours sleep each night. As you plan retreats, trips, and so forth, take into account the resting needs of your early teens and yourself as well. Some years ago on retreats, we started sleeping in on Saturday and Sunday mornings. Wake up was not until 8:30 a.m. I discovered that we still got everything accomplished that we planned and I didn't have cranky teens before the retreat or trip was over. Another thing I discovered was that parents were not on my back for wearing out their teens before they got back home.

These truly are the wonder years—embrace them with your early teens and grow in the grace of God's love.

Chapter 3

The Next Greatest Generation

I was more than ready to give up and walk away from it all. Only three weeks after the Columbine shootings in 1999, a teacher was killed in a shooting at a high school less than two hours away from our church. The youth were coming to youth group with a noticeable fear in their eyes. I had myself convinced that the world was falling apart, and I began to lose hope in this generation. Worse yet, the young people in our group were losing hope. In spite of what they experienced in their own schools, they started to believe the press. The world was falling apart, and they were the generation leading us to destruction.

Then I sat back and took a closer look. I thought about the fifty young people that gathered around the flagpole at the local junior high school—not once a year, but once a month—to pray. I thought about the sixth-grader who came to a church meeting to ask that we skip the bagels and doughnuts once a month and donate the money to a homeless family. I thought about the eighth-grader who led a book drive and collected more than 750 new children's books for a children's shelter in the city. I thought about the public school class that I was invited to speak to about my career in ministry and my calling to serve others. I thought about the junior highs that voted to pass up a ski trip in order to serve lunch at a soup kitchen.

Upon further reflection, the perceptions and myths perpetuated by the media and highlighted by events like Columbine don't hold up against the realities of today's youth culture. What I was seeing on the news was nothing like what I was experiencing in my daily workings with young people. The things that I was hearing from adults about "youth today" did not equate with the testimonies of young people in the church and the public schools. The upbeat and positive nature of today's young people is not limited to the church. In fact, schools are filled with a generation of young people that are generally team oriented, achievement minded, and others focused.

In *Millennials Rising*, Neil Howe and William Strauss warn of a revolution among today's youth—but not the one that doomsayers have expected and portrayed. Instead, they warn of "a good news revolution." The current generation of young people will indeed rebel. They will rebel against the selfishness of their parents' generation by giving more freely of their time, energy, and resources to those in need. They will rebel against failing institutions by rebuilding rather than attacking them. They will rebel against immoral attitudes and behavior among adults by creating a stronger set of morals and values. The greatest danger for this generation will not be the tendency to "do nothing," but the tendency to try to "do everything."

I do want to flash a warning sign before we go further. At the same time that there is an overall "goodness" among today's youth, there are also dangers that lurk in every community around the country. Almost every year since 1993, school violence and suicide rates have declined steadily. However, some young people carry guns to school, and children live in communities where metal detectors are more common than welcome signs. The rate of alcohol and drug abuse has also declined steadily among twelve to eighteen year olds. However, there are eighth-grade graduation parties hosted by parents where alcohol is served because it is "contained." Community volunteerism has become popular, not just because it is mandated by schools but because it is the right thing to do. Yet, young people have and spend more disposable income than any previous generation.

Characteristics of Millennials

Generational experts such as Howe, Strauss, and Craig Kennet Miller point to several key characteristics of the Millennial Generation. In order to minister to today's junior high students we must understand the prevailing winds of the generational shift that will significantly alter the way ministry is done. The challenge will be for Generation X and baby boomer youth leaders who generally abhor structures, fear institutions, and privatize religion to relate with young people who are more trusting, involved, and collaborative. Some of the key characteristics marking the Millennial Generation are:

Hopeful: Unlike their older brothers and sisters of Generation X, Millennials are generally hopeful about the future and encouraged by their ability to make a positive difference in the world. Whereas youth in the eighties and early nineties were skeptical about society and responded by withdrawing into a safer youth culture, Millennials are concerned about the apparent decline in moral and social values and are responding by seeking out ways to make a difference. Today's teenagers want to tackle issues like AIDS, school violence, and drug and alcohol abuse and make a positive contribution to change the course of their future.

Involved: Because of their hopefulness for the future, Millennials want to be involved in shaping that future. A few months ago a friend of mine sat down to dinner with a group of eighth graders at her church. Somehow, the conversation turned to the AIDS epidemic in Africa. As she spoke more about the horrors of how the disease was devastating an entire continent, the students became visibly shaken. "Well, what have you done about it," one young man finally challenged her. Stunned by the directness of the question, she said: "Well, I've written a letter to my representatives asking them to increase support to battle the disease in Africa and I've given money to a few organizations that are serving those who are affected." "That's it," he shot back. "You just got through telling us how awful it was. We can do more." Within forty-five minutes, the young people at the table were planning a campaign to fight AIDS in Africa and talking to the pastor about speaking to the congregation on a Sunday morning. The class has taken on the responsibility of learning the facts about the spread of AIDS in Africa, talking to each Sunday school class about the problem, challenging each member of the church to contact his or her representatives and providing letters for them to use, and collecting money for mission and service agencies. They are leading the congregation by integrating compassion and justice, service and advocacy.

Disagree

Team-oriented: Millennials have been programmed to believe in the value of teamwork. Beginning in kindergarten, children are put into teams where collaborative learning is the standard method of instruction. Many high schools use ropes courses to instill the value of cooperation and team problem solving. Mark Tittley, in an article entitled " Ministry and the Millennial Generation," points out that while the motto for Generation X was "just do it," the motto for Millennials will be "just do it together."

Disagree

Trusting: Millennial teenagers are generally respectful of authority, trusting of their parents, and supportive of their government. Compared with previous generations, these teenagers are not as likely to rebel against the rules and regulations of their parents and teachers. Instead, Millennials are more likely to rebel against the general lack of discipline and moral relativism of older generations. While adults are generally distrusting of governments and institutions, most Millennials believe that they can make a difference by becoming active participants in shaping institutions and structures.

Not too sure. General statement.

Spiritual: The good news is that postmodern young people are highly interested in spirituality as a means for connecting with God. The worship movement of the late nineties points to the desire for Millennials to come into contact with God through religious experience. Praise and worship concerts packed arenas as if for a rock star with young people who were deeply longing for an intimate encounter with the sacred. According to George Barna, the majority of young people continue to identify with the Christian faith (86 percent) and pray to God at least once a week (84 percent). Further, approximately two-thirds of young people continue to participate in church youth groups for fellowship and spiritual development (*Real Teens*, 134–135). One of the greatest challenges for the church is finding ways to connect these young people with authentic Christian experiences rooted strongly in the context of faith communities. A startling wake-up call to the church is that less than 40 percent of young people in youth groups today indicate that they will participate in a church after graduation from high school. Taking into account what George Barna calls "overestimation of future behavior," we can assume that less than one third of young people in youth group today will likely attend a church after leaving home.

> *A startling wake-up call to the church is that less than 40 percent of young people in youth groups today indicate that they will participate in a church after graduation from high school.*

The future in the hands of today's junior high students is indeed bright. But there is still work to be done. The church cannot afford to sit back and allow the hopefulness of today's teens to turn into the despair of many of today's adults. The junior highs in your community and in your church need to hear the good news of Jesus Christ and be transformed into disciples who follow in Christ's footsteps. They need to channel their desire to "do good" into a lifestyle that embodies justice and compassion. They need to convert their desire to be in community into a desire to become the communion of Jesus Christ. The future is bright, but there is work to be done.

Chapter 4
Rethinking Spiritual Formation

"Love the Lord your God with all your heart and with all your soul and with all your mind…Love your neighbor as yourself" (Matthew 22:37-39, NIV).

"And what does the Lord require of you? To act justly and to love mercy and to walk humbly with your God" (Micah 6:8, NIV).

One of the great disservices done by the modern youth ministry movement and the church at large is the fragmentation of the spiritual life. We have unwittingly perpetuated an understanding of spirituality that separates spiritual formation, justice, worship, service, and fellowship. We have different programs that cover different aspects of spirituality and, depending on our own biases, we tend to focus on one area over another.

Over the last several years, the worship movement has swept across the youth ministry landscape. In diverse worship settings, students have a powerful experience of God's presence through music and prayer. These experiences can transform a young person's understanding of God if the experience is connected with an understanding of God's call to serve others in need and work for justice. Similarly, many youth groups focus on works of justice and service without ever making a connection with their inner spiritual transformation.

For junior high youth, the danger and the possibilities are clear. At this point in their development, early adolescents are formulating an understanding of how the world works and how their values fit this design. Just as this is an ideal time to help shape decision-making skills, early adolescence is also a time when the church can shape how young people interpret and live out their relationship with God. Essentially, it is our calling to teach and model an integrated understanding of the spiritual life that encompasses inner transformation, community formation, and acts of justice.

John Wesley talked about "the holiness of heart and life." For Wesley, it was not an option to separate inward holiness and works of mercy and justice. If one were in a relationship with God and being shaped by the disciplines of prayer and Bible study, that person would serve the poor and work for justice to bring about social change. When cornered about "the greatest commandment," Jesus replied with the instruction to love God and neighbor. When posing the question "what does the Lord require?" the prophet Micah insisted that the spiritual life is about justice, mercy, and walking humbly with God. None of these three presents the option for focusing on one area at the expense of another. However, the Christian community and the youth ministry movement have often chosen sides and focused on one area over the other.

One of the easiest ways to avoid this problem is to resist labeling your events as "spiritual formation" or "service projects" or "fellowship nights." Every activity that you do in youth group can and should be connected to the student's relationship with God.

- At the bowling alley, take the time to share prayer concerns and have a student testimony.
- When you are serving in a soup kitchen, take the time to debrief the experience by asking the young people to connect the experience with stories from the Gospels.
- After a powerful worship encounter, ask young people to identify one thing that they will do in school that week to treat someone as Jesus would.

A more difficult, but necessary, step in teaching the integrated spiritual life is evaluating how you are modeling the life of faith. Like it or not, young people are watching how you live much more than they are listening to what you say. Students are watching to see what role God plays in your life. They are looking to see how you connect with God through prayer and Bible study. They are watching how you spend your money and what your priorities are. They are looking at how you deal with the environment and reach out to the poor and outcast of your community. They want to know, more than anything, if this God that you talk about is worth following. They want to know if what you preach on Sunday evening connects with how you live on Tuesday afternoon.

Spiritual Formation and Christian Practices

I was seven years old when I started playing baseball. Every chance I got I was out on a baseball field learning how to catch, throw, hit, or run bases. I started playing catcher at nine and fell in love with the position. So much is required of a catcher. Every play went through me. I controlled the speed of the game and could throw off a batter by my incessant chatter. By age eleven I got all of my own equipment and was playing on two different teams in three seasons. In the winter I worked in the gym on technique and throwing.

At thirteen I began to work with a private tutor who once played on a semi-professional team. Best of all, none of this was forced on me by an overzealous parent. I loved playing and I loved catching.

How many of your students are in a similar situation? They start playing soccer at five years old and are on three different teams by the time they are eight. Or they start playing guitar and spend hours a day learning chords and playing along with the radio. Yet, for some reason, we don't think that junior highs are ready for spiritual practices. Much of junior high ministry is tied to fun and games with a little bit of spirituality thrown in from time to time. Unfortunately this ignores the reality that junior highs are looking for something worth their undying allegiance. They are looking for something that they can commit to. They are looking for something that is worthy of their time, energy, resources, and life.

When we in junior high ministry ignore the spiritual needs of early adolescents and the potential for forming an integrated understanding of the spiritual life, we sell short the young people in our groups. When we make program decisions based on the number of people we can attract rather than the spiritual impact that we can have on a few people, we underestimate the needs and potential of junior highs.

Since the beginning of the Christian movement, spiritual practices have helped to form disciples into the image of Christ. These practices of faith have shaped communities and individuals as followers of Jesus Christ. They are not exercises for spiritual experts, but practices through which all people can receive the gift of God's grace. Just as your junior high students are ready and able to practice soccer for three hours a day, they are also ready to practice their faith. The challenge for the junior high youth worker is to make these practices accessible, developmentally appropriate, and fun.

> *The challenge for the junior high youth worker is to make faith practices accessible, developmentally appropriate, and fun.*

The reality is that people of all ages are ready to experience the practices of faith. In Sunday school, children learn about prayer, worship, meditation, and service. Each night when I put my son to sleep, he prays for his family, his friends and yes, his dinosaurs. He is learning how to practice the faith before he is even aware of the power of prayer. When we take cans and bottles to the recycling bin, he is learning about caring for the environment. When we go to visit a woman from church in a nursing home, he is learning about love and service.

Every time you gather your junior high students together, they are learning about the spiritual life. Even when no explicit curriculum is being taught, certainly implicit curriculum is being lived through your actions and those of the other leaders. In the next few pages, I want to explore a number of different ways that junior high youth can experience spiritual formation through Christian practices. These practices of faith will help young people learn an integrated understanding of the spiritual life. They focus on the inner transformation of souls, outward acts of justice and mercy, and communal acts of worship and praise. For a fuller description of Christian practices that are appropriate for junior highs, see *Way to Live: Christian Practices for Teens*, edited by Dorothy Bass and Don Richter (Upper Room Books, 2002).

Prayer

It never failed. We would gather in a circle to close the meeting in prayer and I would ask for joys and concerns. For the next ten minutes, we would hear about aunts, uncles, neighbors, friends, cats, dogs, parents, and siblings who were in need of God's touch. After everyone had an opportunity to speak his or her concerns, I would ask someone to close in prayer. Undoubtedly, all eyes would fall to the floor and no one would volunteer. I would either end up calling on the same two or three young people or praying myself.

Another friend of mine plays a game where every time his group gathers for prayer, everyone in the group puts their thumbs up to avoid being the last one. The last one to put his or her thumb up has to pray. Unwittingly, we both sent mixed messages about prayer. While we were teaching about the power of prayer and the way prayer brings us into communion with God, we were modeling that prayer was either an art for a select few or a chore to be avoided at all cost. I began to look for ways to teach the power of prayer and make prayer accessible for everyone in the group.

Pray with your eyes open. One of the ways to help junior highs become comfortable with prayer is to have them pray with their eyes open. No, this isn't so that you can look around the room and see who is laughing and cutting up. This is so that you can connect with the other people in the room and remember that God is in your midst. When we gathered in a circle to close in prayer, I would open the circle time to God and ask for other people to speak their joys and concerns. This transforms the more comfortable act of sharing prayer concerns into the prayer itself.

Pray in small groups. Rather than bring the whole group together for prayer, gather them into groups of three or four. I would allow for them to get into their own groups and be with people with whom they are comfortable. Have them share with each other one thing for which they would like the others to pray. Then, ask each person to pray aloud for the person on his or her right.

Pray using liturgy. One of the great ways to have junior highs pray is to use common prayers that you can read together. This not only encourages everyone in the group to pray together, but also reinforces the importance of community prayers. Every couple of months, have the group work on a new group prayer that they can memorize and say together. Ask your pastor to use these prayers in the worship service at different times throughout the year.

In addition to teaching the importance of corporate prayer, help young people to develop personal habits of prayer. One of the greatest things that you can do in junior high ministry is to help every young person in your group find his or her prayer language. During your meetings, explore different forms of prayer and give young people an opportunity to experience prayer. Some ideas include:

- **Use various art forms.** Have young people pray by drawing, sculpting, or painting. Show how creative expression is a prayer without words that relies on feelings and emotions.
- **Use guided meditation.** Allow young people the freedom to use their imagination to pray. Great resources for guided meditation are available in *Deepening Youth Spirituality,* by Walt Marcum, and in *Worship Feast Services,* both from Abingdon Press.
- **Use music.** Junior high youth love music. They can learn to pray by singing, playing an instrument, or even listening to popular music while they focus their hearts on God.
- **Use the mundane.** Help young people tie their prayers to the everyday acts of life. For instance, every time that I brush my teeth I pray for my brothers and their families.

Worship

Worship needs to be an integral part of any junior high ministry. We need to understand worship as those practices that bring us into an encounter with the holy, transcendent God where we can "fall in love, stay in love, and express our love to the God who is smitten with us" (*The Godbearing Life,* 119). In junior high ministry, worship must not be limited to a one-hour experience on Sunday morning or evening. Rather, we must help junior highs understand that worship takes place any time that we intentionally carve out time and space and mark it as holy.

Some of the most incredible worship experiences in my ministry happened at times and places that were unexpected. On one Sunday evening, a snowstorm kept most of the students away from youth group and left us without power. We decided to hold youth group with the four students that lived within walking distance of the church and three leaders. After a great game of sardines, we gathered in the front of the sanctuary where we began to lift up different people in our church and community that were hurting. We shared about our own faith journeys and then began praying for one another. We never sang a song or listened to a sermon, but that worship experience had a tremendous impact on all of us who participated.

Worship in junior high ministry can be part of a planned program or it can happen at unexpected times and places. Authenticity is imperative in worship with junior high youth. Look around you to find those moments that can become an encounter with the Holy. Listen carefully to the needs, hurts, desires, and joys of your youth and make sure they become a part of the worship experience. Most important, involve younger youth in the planning and leadership of worship.

Service

I was amazed at what I saw. Two junior high boys sat across from a homeless man named Micah sharing a hot breakfast. The conversation flowed easily and all three laughed hysterically. When it was almost time to go, I saw them hold hands and pray together. Outside, I told them how thankful I was that they were bold enough to pray for Micah. "Oh," John said, "we didn't pray for him, he prayed for us." "Yeah, he asked us what we were doing for the rest of the day and we told him that we were working at the food bank. Then he asked if he could pray for us," Chris added.

I learned two very important lessons that day. First, never underestimate the capacity of junior highs to be in ministry with others. John and Chris not only ministered to Micah that morning, they also ministered to me. While I struggled through forced conversations with the people we were serving, these two young men engaged in a heart-felt, life-changing exchange. Setting aside barriers of race, age, and socioeconomic status, John and Chris opened their hearts to Micah and he did the same to them. Too often, we limit the types of service that we involve junior highs in because we are not sure they can handle it.

The second lesson I learned was that service is never a one-way street. John and Chris were transformed by the prayers of the very person that they were there to serve. Micah shattered their understanding of service and gave them a greater understanding of the connection of the human family. We do not serve those who are less fortunate than us, we value all people in God's kingdom and act kindly toward our neighbor.

Service is an important part of junior high youth ministry. Developmentally, young people are just beginning to gain the capacity to transform their universe from being "me-focused" to being "others-focused." By involving young people in acts of service we are nurturing that capacity and helping them orient their lives around the needs of others. While service projects are integral to this understanding of faithful living, young people need to learn how they can serve others every day. Not only do youth need to learn how to be servants on a mission trip, they also need to learn how to serve others in their homes, schools, and communities.

There are several ways to involve junior highs in service to others. Some examples include:

Mission trips and service projects. When I first arrived at my last church, there was a long-standing tradition of a senior high service project. Each year, the young people would travel to work with a community organization, a children's home, or Habitat for Humanity. When I presented the idea of a junior high service project to the church board and parents, I was met with a lot of skepticism. "They are not ready for it." "They won't be able to do any real work, they'll just be kept busy." "What will they have to look forward to in senior high?" I carefully answered all of the questions and proceeded with my plans. Needless to say, the trip was an unbelievable success. The children's home where we worked had never had a group who worked so hard and accomplished so much. The youth loved the hard work, the adventure, the devotions, and the relationships that they built with the children at the home. They were engaged, transformed, and excited to go back and serve in our community.

Community projects. One of the greatest outcomes of that first junior high service project was the excitement that the young teens had to serve in our local community. While on the trip, we had great conversations about the different needs that were present in our own area. The youth developed a list of service organizations that they were aware of: soup kitchens, food banks, shelters, and a clothing pantry. When we returned to New Jersey, they created plans to have a monthly service project. They chose the projects, did the planning, and followed through. The impact was felt not only in the community, but also in the church. These junior highs frequently challenged the congregation to be involved in serving the community and offered opportunities for them to be involved.

Random acts of kindness. Challenge your young people to find ways to serve people every day through random acts of kindness. Have them keep a journal for a week listing all of the acts of kindness that they do for another person. Make sure that these random acts of kindness are not public, but something that they do to see all of the ways that they can serve others. Also, make sure that these acts are not something for which they are recognized publicly.

Personal service projects. For confirmation, each young person in the class was required to complete a service project with his or her mentor. They had to identify a need, develop a project, carry out the service, and report about the experience. This was one of the greatest components of the confirmation experience. Junior high students would be involved in tutoring grammar school students, reading at a children's hospital, visiting at a nursing home, and much more. Amazingly, more than 50 percent of the students continued to be involved in the project after the reporting was done. By having to develop the project themselves, they found something that they were passionate about and good at doing.

Works of Justice

As we drove through the neighborhoods of Anacostia, after a day of playing with children in some of the roughest housing projects in Washington D.C., the van was quiet. Above the music on the radio, I overheard a conversation between one of the junior high students and our host from the mission agency. "Why are there so many projects in this one area?" "Because they are cheaper to build here." "Why?" "Because the property value is lower." "Why?" "Because years ago the city planners put a garbage dump, mental institution, and prison on this side of town." Why?" "To keep them away from the tourists who come to see the monuments and museums." Each answer only gave Jennifer more questions. She continued to wrestle with what she saw and heard throughout the day.

The next afternoon, Jennifer got up the courage to go and speak with the woman in charge of running the after-school reading program. "Miss Hawkins," she asked, "I know that it is helpful for us to be here and read books to the children. But, if you could have anything in the world for these children, what would it be?" Quickly the answer came. "For their fathers and mothers to be able to read with them. So many of them are in jail or dead. The ones who aren't have to work three jobs to put food on the table and keep a roof over their head." "Well, what can I do?" "Keep helping, keep asking tough questions, and keep telling our story." Jennifer didn't come away with any easy answers, but she learned that every act of service only addresses the surface of an issue that runs much deeper.

God not only calls us to do works of mercy, but also works of justice. The word of God through the prophet Isaiah is clear: "Learn to do right! Seek justice, encourage the oppressed, defend the cause of the fatherless, plead the case of the widow" (Isaiah 1:17, NIV). It is not enough to salve the wounds of the oppressed if we do not speak out with them and cry for justice and freedom. In youth ministry, we shouldn't bother with works of service if we are not willing to join them with works of justice.

But, how do junior highs wrestle with justice? How can they understand the injustices of society let alone do anything about them? Unfortunately, no simple answers or program ideas can help you conquer the issue of justice.

Justice is not a simple topic. However, there are ways to encourage junior highs to begin thinking about the problems of injustice and raising questions like Jennifer's. Wrestling with these issues in junior high will help formulate the way young people will think and act on these issues in later years.

Identify injustice "at home." Injustice and oppression take on a lot of forms. For junior highs, injustice is not always easy to see, but it is present. Have your students struggle to identify issues of injustice in their own schools and communities.

Dig deeply and ask tough questions. When you involve junior highs in works of service, spend time identifying the critical issues that led to that need. When serving meals in a soup kitchen, be sure to discuss issues of hunger and poverty. Why do so many people in that community not have enough food to eat? Why do some people in the community have so many resources and others have so little? What resources would it take to begin eliminating hunger in the community?

Tackle tough issues. Many of the young people in our churches are sheltered from the horrors of injustice and oppression. At the same time, they need to know how God calls us beyond ourselves to stand with others in the human family who are fighting for freedom and justice. Find an issue that the young people are passionate about and learn how your group can be involved in the struggle. Craig Kielburger was twelve years old when he began his crusade against unfair child labor practices in Third World countries (see *www.freethechildren.org*). Mpule Kwelagobe was thirteen when she began speaking and writing about the pandemic of AIDS on the continent of Africa. Challenge your students to tackle the tough issues. Work with them to learn, to pray, and to find ways to act for justice. Don't underestimate their power. They can make a difference.

Play

One of the most overlooked, yet formative spiritual practices is play. I say overlooked, not because junior high ministry does not involve a tremendous amount of fun and games, but because it is not considered part of spiritual formation. In *Way to Live*, Don Richter and Jack DePaolo wrote a chapter on play that recasts it as a practice of spiritual formation. "Playfulness is a way of being in the world. Playing provides enjoyment, promises freedom, and promotes truth" (*Way to Live*, 128). For junior highs, play can be a release from the pressures of daily life.

Michelle came to youth group every week. Well, at least when she didn't have a tennis match or a soccer game—or if she didn't have too much homework or a rehearsal for the state band—or if she wasn't so exhausted from the week that she fell asleep on Sunday afternoon and didn't wake up until Monday morning. Sadly, a lot of junior high students are just like Michelle. Every minute of their day is programmed and they are pushed to succeed and excel at everything they do. Youth group is an ideal place to help free young people from the demands of their lives and experience an oasis.

When viewed as a spiritual practice, play can have a tremendous impact on your students' well-being. But we must be careful to define play in a way that is fun and free, not structured and competitive. Here are some tips for play:

Play games in which everyone can participate. Of course, softball is a game that everyone can play. You can have forty people in the game at any given time. But, most likely, you will have about eight youth actually playing and the others running from the ball and avoiding participation at all costs. Make sure that the games you play have a role for everyone. Avoid games that are tests of skill, strength, or power.

Play games without rules. Have you ever spent thirty minutes trying to explain a game that lasted for thirty seconds? I have and it's a disaster. The youth quickly become bored with the rules and tune them out. The game begins and no one knows how to play. The game usually ends with someone getting hurt or me getting frustrated. Learn to play games with no rules. Better yet, encourage your young people to remember their childhood and use their imaginations to create new games.

Play team games with a common goal. One of the worst things a junior higher can experience is to be singled out in a game or sport and fail. Most junior highs are uncomfortable with their size, their looks, and their physical ability. Many are awkward and clumsy. You'd be surprised how many young people choose not to come to youth group for fear of being embarrassed during a game. Find games where a group of students must work together to accomplish a goal. Group games and low rope courses are great ways for students to play without feeling singled out or uncomfortable.

You do not have to sacrifice fun for spiritual formation in junior high ministry. Having fun and fellowshipping can be transforming and powerful for the lives of junior highs. Be careful not to set a tone of separation between fun and faith. Encourage holy habits in the lives of your youth and empower them to live out their faith.

Junior High Youth and Service Projects

by Jim Bielefeldt

Although I had been involved with junior high ministry for more than fifteen years at the time, I always avoided taking the junior high group on a service project. That is, nothing longer than a weekend project that was within twenty miles of the church! All of that changed in 1995 when I helped lead the first group of twenty junior high youth on a week-long project to a children's home and orphanage about 250 miles from our church. We really did not know what to expect on this inaugural trip. While we had a history of more than twenty-five years of senior high service projects, this was a whole new experience for us. A lot of prayer, a great team of advisors, and a ton of diet soda with caffeine saw us through the first project and it turned out to be an overwhelming success!

Since that initial trip we have taken our junior high on a week-long service project each summer. I have found that there are far more pros than cons with these trips and I would like to share some of the lessons learned for me during these trips. But first, I want to share some myths that were shattered with the first couple of trips.

Myths Proven Untrue

Myth: Junior high students are not ready for a week-long service project.

Junior high students are more than ready for a long service project! We have found that the sixth- through eighth-grade students are very capable of handling a week away from their homes. They know that the project is not a vacation, but a time of serious commitment both to the project at hand and to the group as well.

Myth: Junior high students are not capable of working hard for one full day, let alone five!

This myth was proven false with our first project and totally shattered with our second and third. Each time, the students worked harder than we anticipated and willingly served with their hands and their hearts.

Myth: Junior high students are not capable of leading vacation Bible schools and similar programs.
Not only have we witnessed junior high students stepping up to this challenge, but we have also had to have them improvise VBS lessons one week when we learned that we were scheduled to deliver a program—with less than twenty minutes notice. It is amazing how creative junior high students can be when they are faced with a challenge.

Myth: Junior high leaders have to be crazy to want to take students on week-long trips!
OK, crazy helps since you need to really love junior high youth to spend a full week, 24/7 with them! But trust me, you will receive so much more in return for this one week investment.

As mentioned earlier, many pros and cons have been learned. The ones below come from a few years experience. I am sure that many of you could add to both sections of these lists.

Pros

Opportunities to minister: Spending a week with youth offers you incredible opportunities to minister with them one on one, in small groups, and in a large group setting. Standing next to one of your youth shoveling mulch for five hours or spending the afternoon making sandwiches for the homeless persons offers you a chance to share your faith with the youth and allows them a comfortable setting to open up to you and share some of their faith story with you.

Community building: Nothing is better, or quicker, in bringing a group together than a service project. Evening debriefing sessions, group team-building activities, and close-quarter living go a long way in unifying a group in a short period of time. Service projects give you an opportunity to pair the quiet, reserved youth with that boisterous, in-your-face one with results that can produce friendships and bonds that last for a long, long time.

Love and learn: A week with your youth gives you an opportunity to show them God's love and your love for them individually. Many of the youth who have joined us on a project have a desperate need to feel God's love in their lives. Having a chance to show them how they are making a difference each and every day allows them to feel that love firsthand. You have the opportunity to see inside the heart of each of your youth and learn what each of them needs from you to help them in their relationship with Jesus Christ.

Daily devotions: I have participated in projects where the sponsoring group will prepare daily devotions. I personally prefer to do my own, and I have found that most groups will allow you to do your own on a daily basis. I like to incorporate things that happened during the day with the evening devotions and I make sure that the message being delivered will help the group with any issues that they are facing such as cliques, focusing on purpose, relationships. I have also tried to offer the youth an optional Bible study every morning. This gives those youth who want to spend extra time studying the Word an opportunity to do so. I have always been amazed at the number of youth who *choose* to participate and come faithfully every day!

Serving others: Obviously the main point of going on a service project is to serve the Lord and to serve others. I have found that God has always guided us to the right project for our group at a particular time. We have served in urban settings and in the backwoods of the country, building a new church. Although lots of organizations offer a variety of projects, I have found that setting up your own project for your group can be very rewarding. Find a children's home, a church camp, or some other setting where your group could use their particular skills.

Cons

A group divided: While a service project can unbelievably unite those on the project, make sure that, upon your return to the church, you help those who did not attend still feel a part of the group. It is easy for those who went on the project to view the event as a mountaintop experience and, at times, to make those who did not attend feel excluded. An effort is needed to bring the unity that occurred during the project to those back at home who were unable to attend.

Focusing on the trip, not the Lord: The focus can sometimes move away from your purpose and onto problems. You feel that you are not accomplishing as much as you should; you have trouble uniting the group; your group is tired and overwhelmed. When these things occur it is important to refocus on your purpose — serving the Lord and accomplishing what the Lord wants you to accomplish.

One of our first junior high service projects, we went into a rural area to help rebuild a church that had been destroyed in a fire. The building site had been cleared and our job was to install a new Styrofoam form system for the foundation. What was involved was placing more than a thousand foam partitions totally around the perimeter approximately eight-feet high. The forms were tied together with plastic stays and bailing twine.

After three days of very hard labor you could literally see the foundation of the new church on the site. It was very rewarding to see the fruits of your labors so clearly before you. At around 4:00 that afternoon, a huge windstorm blew into the area, and we watched all of our hard work collapse around us like a house of cards. When the storm was finished so was all the work we had accomplished since the start of the trip. All we could do is stare, wide-eyed and in shock, and begin to cry. Our faith was truly tested at this moment. Many felt that the project was over, that we might as well pack up and go home. Many felt that the work they had accomplished was all in vain.

Thinking quickly, the youth pastor gathered the group and related the story from Luke 8, about Jesus calming the storm and chastising the disciples for having such little faith. He then went on to point out to us all that we did accomplish on the trip up to that point. The group rallied around his words of inspiration and went on to rebuild the complete foundation system in less than a day and a half! We don't know why God sent that storm, and a few others, to us during that trip, but we do know that the youth learned and grew from each of those storms and left that trip with a faith that will be able to weather many storms in their lives.

I encourage you to seriously consider adding a junior high service project to your schedule. The rewards far outweigh the risks and the returns are definitely worth the investment.

Chapter 5

From Catacombs to Catechesis

The blank faces staring back at me were disturbing in and of themselves. Then came the yawns, the glazed eyes, the bobbing head, and eventually the snoring. Granted the material I was trying to cover was not the most exciting stuff in the world (you try teaching Church polity to a roomful of thirteen year olds), but I thought I was a better teacher than that. Needless to say, my first experience with teaching confirmation was not a grand success. In many ways the Sunday school class felt like a cold catacomb. No, the students weren't dead—yet. But there was certainly very little life at that moment.

Having just graduated college with a degree in youth ministry, I called one of my mentors from an internship I had completed the previous summer. "Dale, this is Drew. Confirmation class is a disaster. You have to help me find a way to teach this information in a way that will keep their interest. I'm dying out there!" After a pensive sigh and a thoughtful pause, my mentor addressed my question. "Confirmation is not about instruction, it is about catechesis. You are not trying to make sure that every youth gets all of the information, you are trying to pass on the mantle of faith." "Great," I thought to myself, "that will really help next week!" The conversation continued and I learned a lot as I sat humbly at my mentor's feet. Of course, what I really wanted was a great lesson plan for the following week but what I got was crumbs that led me down a long pathway to discovery.

Kenda Creasy Dean and Ron Foster define catechesis in terms of "expanding faith." The process of passing on the Christian faith, they argue, is similar to that of a midwife breaking a mother's water. Every time we push young people to a deeper understanding of faith or cause ripples in their understanding, we are catechists—bringing about birth and new life. "Catechesis means oral teaching. It implies an intentional transmission (teaching) in the most accessible way possible (talking about faith) . . . Simply put, catechesis means telling others about the Christian tradition" (*Godbearing Life*, 162). Along my journey of discovery, I have learned several things about catechesis.

Catechesis is about a person, not a program. *The Godbearing Life* begins with this profound statement: "The most important thing about Christianity isn't 'what' but 'Who.' The most important thing about youth ministry isn't 'what' but 'Who.'" Our focus in teaching junior highs should not be about passing on information (what) that they may or may not incorporate into their daily lives. Our focus should be on becoming Christlike and transmitting the faith so that young people can become like Christ (Who).

As catechists (teachers), our job is to embody Christ so that youth will experience the transforming power of God's grace through us. In order to do that, we must be in a relationship with Christ that is alive and growing.

> *Curriculum does not teach, teachers teach.*

We have access to scores of great curriculum resources for junior high ministry (see page 91), and they are helpful tools. However, let us be very clear—curriculum does not teach, teachers teach. Who you are with young people says a lot more than what you say.

Catechesis is a process, not a product. We have no clear end result to the act of passing on the Christian faith. Like Paul, we want our students to mature and "put on the fullness of Christ." But, if we are honest, we know that we are not fully mature ourselves. Passing the mantle of faith is less about the information we teach and more about the way we teach—and *live*—the information.

The Christian faith is not as much learned as it is lived. Young people learn about the lifelong journey of discipleship as they walk side by side with peers and caring adults. Rather than leading young people to a destination, our job is to give them tools for the journey. Teaching Bible studies are important, but it is more important to teach junior highs how to study the Bible. Praying together is important, but it is more important to teach young people how to pray. Asking the tough questions of youth is important, but it is more important to help young people learn how to question for themselves.

Catechesis involves pilgrims, not pupils. The students in your junior high ministry are not learners sitting on the receiving end of your wisdom. They are fellow pilgrims who are on a different place in their faith journey. Certainly pastors, youth leaders, and parents have incredible things to teach junior highs about life and faith. But, we also have an incredible amount to learn as we journey alongside the young people with whom we are in ministry.

Catechesis is prickly, not palatable. Passing on the Christian faith is not about making students comfortable with being a Christian so that they adopt our faith and values. Catechesis involves walking with students through the rough places of their lives. We cannot teach a class or lead a youth group without being aware of the students in our groups who are dealing with divorce, death, or depression. We must not be afraid to enter the briar patch of early adolescence and deal with their most difficult and pressing issues. To do so would not only lose credibility with the young people, but also it would be unfaithful to the Christ who abandoned the throne of heaven to walk in our shoes.

Another challenge about the comfort offered by many middle and upper-middle class youth groups comes from Michael Warren, author of *Youth, Gospel, and Liberation*. In a speech, Warren declared his concern that the vision of Jesus commonly presented to middle-class youth is that of a middle-class Jesus who represents the causes and concerns of a privileged society. The emphasis, Warren points out, tends to be on Jesus as the one who comforts rather than the one who confronts and challenges injustice in society. He issues a call for youth workers to embrace Jesus in the lives of the poor, weak, and outcast. What we seek to pass on to early adolescents is not a moral framework for righteous living but a Christian framework for Kingdom living. The Kingdom of God is about welcoming the stranger, befriending the outcast, and loving the poor. Junior high ministry must help young people move beyond themselves into a world where justice and mercy are lived out in their relationships at school, in church, and in their community.

> *Rather than leading young people to a destination, our job is to give them tools for the journey.*

Sunday School and Bible Study

Whenever I lead a workshop on junior high ministry, I inevitably face the question "what curriculum do I use for Sunday school?" While I have offered several suggestions for curriculum (page 91), I must reinforce that teaching the faith is not merely a matter of curriculum. I have seen great teachers who were given poor curriculum who have captured the attention and the imagination of their students. Likewise, I have seen great curriculum misused by people who are simply looking for enough material to fill an hour and keep students entertained. Teaching the Bible and passing on the faith to junior highs involves an investment of time, energy, and creativity. If we attempt to sleepwalk through a lesson—which I admit doing on a number of occasions—we will not only bore students, but we dishonor God with our nonchalance.

Duffy Robbins, in his book *Ministry of Nurture*[1], points to seven laws of teaching that he derived from John Milton Gregory. These principles must serve as the backbone to our understanding of the ministry of teaching. They are not program ideas, but values that will inform and direct all of our teaching with junior highs.

Law 1—The law of the teacher. A few weeks ago, I got into a conversation with my four-year-old son about bees. No, not *the birds and the bees*, just bees. His sister had just been stung and Jeremy wanted to know why bees would sting people. I tried to answer his innocent questions and before long I was talking about the worker bees' competition for the approval of the queen bee and their subsequent battles that lead to increased anger that eventually led to Allison being stung. It was obvious to me—and judging by his face, to him—that I had no idea what I was talking about.

Have you ever gotten in to a similar situation with a junior high student while teaching Bible study? I have. What starts out as a lesson we are completely prepared for is sidetracked by a faith-shattering, life-shaping question that I have no idea how to answer. The law of the teacher means that we must actually know the subject that we teach. Does this mean that we have all of the answers? No. It simply means that we cannot be teachers of the Bible if we are not first students of the Bible. Young people must see that you are committed to studying the Scripture and applying it to your own life before they will be able to hear the lessons that you teach.

> *We cannot be teachers of the Bible if we are not first students of the Bible.*

Law 2—The law of the learner. When I stood in front of the confirmation class attempting to teach United Methodist polity, the problem was not the material that I was using as much as it was my inability to capture the interest of the students. The law of the learner states that the learner must be interested (or made to be interested) in the subject being learned. Simple enough, that's why we put ice breakers and games at the beginning of every lesson plan. The problem is that these activities only hold students' attention for the duration of an activity. Once we move on to the heart of our lesson, they have moved on to something else as well. We must create an atmosphere where students are excited to learn and wanting to know more. Sometimes this can happen with an incredible opening game or activity. Sometimes it means taking the students off-site to a surprise location where they can use all of their senses to explore the topic (for example, going to a lake to study baptism). Whatever the approach, the key is to shatter the students out of the know-it-all mode and open them up to new experiences of learning.

Law 3—The law of language. One of my best friends, Jim, has a dog named Chester. Jim and Chester have an incredible relationship. I am amazed every time that I am with them that they have developed a common language. Jim can grunt, and Chester will jump into his lap. Chester will moan, and Jim will go get the leash. The last time I was at their house, I sat in Jim's chair and grunted. Chester just stared at me like I was crazy. When I heard

Chester moan, I immediately reached for the leash. Chester growled at me and barked very disapprovingly. Obviously, I didn't understand their language.

Sadly, many junior high youth feel the way that I did when it comes time to study the Bible. They may want to study the Bible with us but they do not understand the language. It's not just about Bible translations, although that is an important discussion. It is about whether or not we can develop a common language for studying the Scripture. As a teacher, you need to be willing and able to speak the language of your youth and relate the message of Christ in their vernacular.

Law 4—The law of the lesson. When she was two years old, my daughter Allison burned her hand on grandma's curling iron. Now, every time she reaches for something hot we remind her of that experience and she quickly pulls her hands away. The principle behind the law of the lesson is simple—truth being taught must be learned through a truth already known. There is no way that we could convince Allison to stay away from hot things until she understood what hot really was. We need to understand that there is a sequential nature of catechesis. Teaching about spiritual gifts before young people learn about the Holy Spirit is illogical. Teaching about the Resurrection before teaching about the Crucifixion is groundless. Like building a house, we must begin with a foundation before adding walls and eventually a roof.

Law 5—The law of the teaching process. Simply put, this means that we learn best what we discover on our own. Mrs. Pietrucha, my eighth grade physical science teacher, understood this very well. When we were studying ecosystems, we took field trips to swamps, beaches, and forests. When we were studying plants, we went to a greenhouse. When we were studying gravity, we dropped eggs from the roof of the school. Truthfully, the best teachers that I had in junior high school were the ones that encouraged me to find answers to my own questions before I even asked them. This learner-centered approach is also applicable for Bible study and Sunday school. Rather than lay out the theological truths in a Bible passage, give your students the tools to dig for truths themselves. Encourage the use of creativity—drama, music, art, interpretive dance, poetry—to help young people explore the Bible and find the truth that is waiting for them.

Law 6—The law of the learning process. "OK," I said at the conclusion of the class, "who can sum up today's lesson?" A few hesitant hands raised around the room. ".Jesus loves us?" "God is good?" "Jesus wept?" Obviously, they had totally missed the point of the lesson on the parable of the good Samaritan. Perhaps this is a bit too far-fetched, but it points to the principle behind the sixth law: Students must be able to reproduce the truth being learned. This

From Catacombs to Catechesis

does not mean that students can merely summarize the lesson they just heard. Rather, it means that they must be able to internalize the lesson and apply it to their own lives. What is God calling them to do differently as a result of what they have learned? How is God calling them to act toward other people? How would they explain this lesson to a friend? All of these questions can help us probe whether or not students truly grasped the lesson.

Law 7—The law of review and application. For weeks my wife and I taught our son his phone number and address. Every night we would go over the information and he would say it at least three times. One day in school, Jeremy's class had a police officer visit. He asked them how many of them knew their phone number and address. Jeremy confidently raised his hand and gave the officer the information. He received a sticker for his great work, but the greater reward was the pride he felt for knowing this information. That experience taught us firsthand about the law of review and application—in order to retain a learned truth, students must learn through repetition and application. I'm sorry to say that junior highs will not learn about the value of serving others through one Bible study. In fact, it may take them years worth of Bible studies and several weeks worth of hands on service. But, when given the opportunity to review and apply what they learn, service can become part of who they are throughout their lives.

[1] "The Magnificent Seven Laws of Teaching" are reprinted from The Ministry of Nurture, copyright © 1990 by Youth Specialties, Inc., 300 South Pierce Street, El Cajon, CA 92020; *www.YouthSpecialties.com.* Used by permission.

Confirmation

Many faith traditions incorporate the rite of confirmation into their catechetical ministry with early adolescents. Confirmation is a rite of the church that celebrates a young person's decision to claim the faith of the church as his own. Although it might also be coupled with membership in the local congregation, it is first and foremost an act of faith as a young person embraces baptismal vows. The following are some suggestions for enlivening your confirmation ministry:

Focus on the journey, not the ritual. Confirmation is a process that helps prepare young persons for the lifelong journey of Christian discipleship. In many cases, parents, pastors, and church leaders perpetuate an understanding of confirmation as a one-time event that youth have to do in order to satisfy their responsibilities to the church. Many young people are forced in to confirmation programs against their will. While that is not the ideal situation, it does provide an opportunity for you to break down some of those myths and help young people wrestle with their understanding of the Christian faith.

One of the greatest gifts that you can give young people in this process is the freedom of knowing that their commitment to Christ at confirmation is one step in a lifelong journey of discipleship. You are not preparing them for Confirmation Sunday; you are preparing them to live as a follower of Christ.

Encourage questioning and discovery. Confirmation is a time when young people, who are just beginning to develop the ability to think abstractly, wrestle with the deepest issues of faith and life. As they grapple with their faith, they will inevitably ask questions that challenge you and push you toward new discovery. Do not simply provide the answers and attempt to move on. Instead, encourage questioning and provide the tools for young people to discover their own answers.

Involve young people in service and missions. Part of living a life of discipleship is being involved in serving others. As young people discover what the Christian faith is all about, engage them in service and missions. You can do a service project as a class or you can ask students to develop their own service projects. Regardless, the important part is helping young people understand the role of servanthood in the life of faith.

Involve the entire congregation in confirmation. At baptism, congregations pledge to be a part of raising children in the Christian faith. Likewise, confirmation should be viewed as the ministry of the entire congregation. Involve committees, women's groups, trustees, church staff, and other groups in the confirmation program by having them host monthly breakfast for the confirmands. The groups can get to know the young people in the class and share a little bit about the ministries in which they are involved. Similarly, the confirmands can provide snacks for church meetings, help the trustees with a painting project, or send notes of encouragement to the church staff.

Pair young people with an adult mentor. Young people need to develop spiritual friendships with adults who are living out the Christian faith. More than information, they need role models who are walking with Jesus Christ. Encourage the students and mentors to study the Bible together, pray together, serve together, and have fun together. Provide resources and training to help the mentors feel comfortable in their role.

Avoid the "graduation" syndrome. Consider holding confirmation in the fall, not the spring. When I first suggested this to the leadership at my church, I was told that confirmation "was always on Pentecost." However, we had been wrestling with the fact that many young people, regardless of what we were teaching, viewed confirmation as a sort of graduation. It was more than a coincidence that the confirmation service was always held within two weeks of their eighth-grade graduation. By moving confirmation into the fall, we were able to help students connect into the senior high youth program and model the understanding of confirmation as a beginning rather than ending.

From Catacombs to Catechesis

Help students prepare a statement of faith. At the end of the confirmation journey, help young people write a statement of their faith. This is not intended to be a final thesis of their faith, but a statement of where they are at this point on their journey. Have the statements available for the congregation to read in the weeks before and after confirmation. You may even publish them in the church's newsletter. When students are in their senior year of high school, encourage them to write another faith statement. You can have them compare the two statements and see how much they have grown in their understanding of the Christian faith.

Catechesis or Christian education does not have to leave you and your youth feeling like you're wandering in the catacombs. You can have an exciting teaching ministry simply by meeting the youth where they are educationally and involving them in the learning process. Focus less on the individual lessons and more on the big transformation picture when you plan your Bible studies, Sunday school curriculum, and confirmation programs. Develop a master plan for passing on the faith to your youth instead of giving them snack-sized portions of spiritual information here and there. Put as much energy into Christian education as you do to your next lock-in or retreat. Again, you do not have to be a spiritual expert, but youth require authenticity and stay involved and interested if they can sense their spiritual growth. For more information on developing a master plan, go to *www.ileadyouth.com*. You can choose from different plans, or learn to form your own.

My Faith Statement

by Liz Bielinski

Over the past year in confirmation class, I have learned so much about myself and my relationship with God. I grew up in church, participating in church choir, bell choir, and knowing as much as I thought that I needed to know about God and the Bible. Soon, I grew to realize that there was more to being a Christian than saying prayers before bed and going to church on Sunday morning. I never really had a personal relationship with God until the junior youth fellowship trip to Washington D.C., the summer after my seventh grade.

There, in the inner city of D.C., was the first time that I ever really felt the overwhelming power of God's love. The devotions, the service, and the friendships helped me to experience God. God was in the hands of those strangers that I had grasped on the street, in the eyes of the children in Anacostia, and in the hearts of those who stood around me every day. Accepting God into my life has changed me in ways that I never knew were possible. I was always a generally good kid, but until my God experience something had been missing. Ever since that time two-and-a-half years ago, I have become a different person. I no longer jump to conclusions about people, nor am I so quick to lose my faith when something bad happens in my life. I am now able to understand that God works in my life in mysterious ways.

One of my favorite songs by Steven Curtis Chapman talks about the change that happens in us when we claim Christ as our Lord. I love the part about making my life show that I'm in the process of the change. The lyrics show exactly what happened to me after the JYF service project. I realized that if I wanted to live the life that God wants me to I would have to show the change. I can't have a Christian life without changing some of my actions. Along with the love that Christians show, I must have grace, hope, and forgiveness to complete the puzzle. This song helps me to see how I can allow God to change me so that I am living the life that Christ wants me to.

Throughout my life I have come across many trials that could have caused me to lose my faith if it had not been for the constant strength in my life, God. God is my rock, my foundation, and my everything. God has blessed me with friends and family who will stand by me no matter what. God has blessed me with a church family that has surrounded me with love and acceptance. I can face my problems when I turn to God. I have realized that if I need strength, I can turn to God and I will be safe in the arms of Love. Another of my favorite songs by Steven Curtis Chapman talks about having an attitude of "bringing it on." The song says to let the storms rise and hard times come, but let me rely on the strength of Christ. These words are a constant source of comfort to me. This song helps me to realize that no matter what comes my way, I don't have to be afraid because I always have God behind me helping me through it all. "The Lord upholds all those who fall and lifts up all who are bowed down. The eyes of all look to you, and you give them their food at the proper time. You open your hand and satisfy the desires of every living thing. The Lord is righteous in all ways and loving toward all he has made. The Lord is near to all who call on him, to all who call on him in truth" (Psalm 145:14-18, NIV). God is my refuge and my strength in all the storms of life.

Chapter 6

The Undiscovered Treasure: Junior Highs and Leadership

"But the LORD said to Samuel, 'Do not consider his appearance or his height, for I have rejected him. The LORD does not look at the things man looks at. Man looks at the outward appearance, but the LORD looks at the heart'"
(1 Samuel 16:7, NIV).

In his search for a king of Israel, Samuel found himself at the house of Jesse where God instructed him that he would anoint one of Jesse's sons. The proud father paraded his sons before Samuel assured that he would be pleased with such a fine assemblage of strength, courage, and leadership. Eliab was first—tall, healthy looking, strong—everything that a nation could hope for or want in a king. But, Eliab was not God's chosen. Then Abinadab, Shammah, and the rest of the boys were brought out one by one. But the favor of the Lord did not rest on any of them. Frustrated, Jesse called for his youngest son David who was tending sheep out in the pasture. When he arrived from the fields Samuel anointed him as the future king—in spite of his young, boyish appearance.

The story of David's anointing is not unlike the experience of many junior high youth in the church. Their leadership potential is easily overlooked in favor of their older, more "prepared" senior high counterparts. Often, many junior high ministries don't include a leadership component for students. In addition, many junior high youth are not considered for different leadership opportunities in the church. Unfortunately, in this is case everyone loses. When junior highs are not given the chance to develop their leadership potential in the church, the church misses out on the unique gifts that junior highs bring to the tasks they undertake. When churches invest time and energy into developing young leaders—beginning with junior highs—the young people and the church benefit.

Developmental Tasks and Leadership

When thinking about junior highs and leadership, remember the developmental tasks and needs of these early adolescents. Young people need to be put into leadership situations that are developmentally appropriate and that will nurture their leadership potential. We need to avoid situations that could have a negative impact on their psychosocial and leadership development.

Developing peer relationships: One of the key developmental tasks of early adolescents is the formation of peer networks. Early adolescence is a time when young people begin to become dependent on peer relationships and have a need to form strong bonds with others outside of their families. Any approach to leadership with junior highs must take into account this critical need. Rather than identify leaders who stand out from the group, create a leadership team that works together with the whole group on developing a strong ministry. Further, junior high leaders can be trained most effectively in a group environment where they can develop healthy relationships and learn to rely on the strengths of others in the group.

> *Create a leadership team that works together with the whole group on developing a strong ministry.*

Not only is this approach more developmentally appropriate, it also provides a biblical model for leadership that avoids the super-leader syndrome. Throughout the letters of Paul, we are reminded that the church is a "body," and each part receives different gifts to carry out the work of Christ in the world. Most attempts at leadership development in youth ministry, however, call for a few key students to shoulder the load. Often, this leaves young people who develop certain leadership traits such as public speaking and communication skills overburdened. More disturbingly, it promotes a perception that the most effective leaders are loud and outgoing and ignores the leadership potential of youth with other, less outwardly noticeable gifts.

Developing decision-making skills: Other key developmental tasks of early adolescents include developing the skills and acquiring the freedom to make decisions. These tasks raise two key factors for junior high leadership. First, at this critical stage young people will formulate ideas about leadership and decision making that will continue into adulthood. This is an ideal time to teach group decision-making and consensus-building skills that can create community among student leaders and their peers. Rather than placing the focus on the decision itself, this is a time to help young leaders learn a healthy process for making decisions.

Second, junior highs need to be given the freedom to make important decisions about program content, mission opportunities, retreat destinations, and more. It is not appropriate to bring junior highs together for leadership development without giving them opportunities to exercise those gifts. If you are making room for junior high youth at the leadership table, make sure the adults nurture the leadership instead of taking over and making all the decisions themselves.

Forming identity: Early adolescents are at a point when they begin to answer the question, "Who am I?" Most of the time, younger youth do not include leadership in their formation of self-identity. Leaders are "the other kid" who fits more of the characteristics adolescents commonly associate with leadership — self-confidence, extroversion, popularity, intelligence, physical fitness, and so forth. However, leadership is not something that should be set aside for a few select individuals. When given the opportunity, all teenagers can learn necessary skills to be a leader among other teenagers and adults. Churches can help young people embrace their own leadership potential and provide an atmosphere where that potential can be nurtured.

> *When given the opportunity, all teenagers can learn necessary skills to be a leader among other teenagers and adults.*

What Junior Highs Bring to Leadership

Junior highs bring many positive qualities to the art of leadership. When given opportunities to lead that are developmentally appropriate and put in positions that will yield success, junior highs will shine as leaders in your youth ministry and the wider church.

Available: One of the strengths that junior highs bring to leadership is their availability. Compared to many senior high youth, junior high students have more free time that is not programmed with school and extracurricular activities. This allows for more time for leadership training and mentoring.

Moldable: Even though peer approval is very important, early adolescents are very open to the input of significant adults in their lives. When adults in the church take the time to mentor junior highs in the art of leadership, they are likely to incorporate those learned skills into their personality.

Faithful: I have consistently found that when I invest time, energy, and resources into developing junior high leaders, they are faithful to the youth ministry and the church. Place your trust in junior highs and encourage them by giving them both the opportunity to succeed and the freedom to fail.

Creative: No doubt, junior high youth have an incredible ability to think through problems and arrive at creative solutions. Unlike adults and even senior highs, they are not bound by "what we've always done before." Give junior highs the opportunity to wrestle with difficult issues. Offer input and wisdom from your experience but allow them the freedom to use their creativity to arrive at solutions.

Energetic: A standing joke among leaders of junior high ministry is that you have to be able to play three hours of games, worship for two hours, eat for two hours, go bowling, play sardines until 4:00 in the morning, and then have an in-depth discussion about faith and salvation. Well, the same energy that junior highs bring to lock-ins and other events, they will bring to the responsibilities of leadership.

Along with all of the positive characteristics that junior highs bring to leadership, some challenges exist as well. These challenges are not obstacles that should prevent you from incorporating leadership development into your youth ministry, but things that you need to be conscious about as you begin.

> *When junior highs invest in leadership, they will be faithful and committed.*

Unpredictable: Mary was an eighth grader who babysat for us on a regular basis. She was trained in CPR, trustworthy, and generally reliable. Every Tuesday night she would meet me at the church and watch our son while I participated in a senior high Bible study. On one of the weeks when I was to lead the study, Mary didn't show up. I called her house and found out that she was with a friend at the mall. She was not being irresponsible and blowing me off, she was being an early adolescent. Adults must remember that although junior highs have incredible capacity for leadership, they also are at a stage when they are me-focused and unpredictable. We have all seen students who can lead worship one moment and wreak havoc the next. Rather than use negative reinforcement and show our disappointment when a student makes a mistake, we must reinforce the positive aspects of their leadership potential and help them grow from their mistakes. For instance, rather than calling Mary to vent my frustration and heap on guilt or shame, I wrote her a note that simply said: "Thanks for all that you do in our ministry. I appreciate the time that you give to watch Jeremy while I lead senior high Bible study. I will see you next week!" Sure enough, she returned next week and every week after that.

Emotional: One of the great things about junior highs is that when they invest in leadership, they will be faithful and committed. The only downside to that commitment is that they will also feel success and failure very deeply. As you work with junior highs on a project, be certain to prepare them for different possible outcomes. If they plan an outreach event for two hundred people and only twenty-five show up, they will be devastated. That could be an incredible learning experience if they are prepared to deal with the emotions they will certainly feel. Help them understand that success is not defined only by numbers, and that God is pleased with their faithfulness in ministry.

Do's and Don'ts of Junior High Leadership

Do incorporate every student in leadership. Each of the students in your youth group has leadership potential. Find creative ways to involve each of your students in some type of leadership role. Whether it is teaching a Bible study or taking pictures on the retreat, every junior high student should have some opportunity to develop their leadership potential. Not only will you then allow students to take ownership of the ministry, you will also help them reshape what they define as leadership.

Don't hold elections. One of the easiest ways to form a leadership team is to hold elections. Personally, I am not in favor of elections for any youth group. This form of leadership selection can be particularly damaging for early adolescents. Junior highs are already at a place when they feel vulnerable and often question their self-worth. Elections can often damage the emotional development of a young person who feels called to leadership but is not affirmed by their peers because they lack the popularity, looks, or other external leadership qualities.

Do help young people identify their gifts for leadership. Several tools can be useful in helping junior highs identify their particular gifts for leadership. Spiritual gift inventories for adolescents can be found on the Web or through a youth resources catalog. You can also develop an "interest inventory" to find out what areas appeal to each student. This not only helps to match young people with leadership roles that they enjoy and are gifted for, but also helps steer clear of the common mistake of putting young people with perceived gifts in positions where they will lose interest and possibly fail.

Don't patronize. Usually, everyone I talk to wants to involve junior highs in leadership. The problem is that many people are not ready to let go of control enough to allow the young people to make significant decisions. You need to be ready and willing to allow junior highs to steer the ship, even when you don't necessarily like the direction it is going. Of course, this doesn't mean that you shouldn't continue to be a spiritual guide and companion on the journey. It simply means that you can't ask junior highs to lead and then control all of the strings.

Do use mentoring. The most effective way to help young people develop their leadership potential is to pair them with someone who can help shape their understanding. A good mentor does not need to be a part of your ministry program, but must be willing to invest some time and energy into the young person's life. Most recently, a young man from our group took on the responsibility for the monthly newsletter. I asked a man from the church who works for the city newspaper to work with him as he got started. They not only developed a friendship and grew together spiritually, but I had a great newsletter!

Don't put the expectations out of reach for most students. Many of my friends use an application process and have strict guidelines for what it means to be a student leader. While I think this approach has merit for finding the strongest leaders in a group, it also ignores the leadership potential of the majority of students. We've already said that most students don't identify themselves as leaders because they don't think they measure up to an external set of standards. When we create another set of standards that is difficult to achieve, we set aside scores of potential leaders. Every student has the potential to be a leader. When given the opportunity, most students will take advantage of the chance to be a part of a leadership team. It usually works out that the more a student can commit to leadership development, the greater potential will be realized. A student who can only commit to an hour a week should be given an opportunity to have a leadership role appropriate to that level of commitment in the same way that a student who can commit to five hours a week should.

> *Every student has the potential to be a leader.*

Junior high youth are ripe for leadership. Because they are at such an incredible stage of life, you can help them form skills for leading, mentoring, and even just participating with enthusiasm. The importance of finding leadership opportunities for everyone in your group is imperative. Help them feel like you are a team of Christians in ministry together. Empower and equip them to be servants to the world.

Junior Highs and Leadership

by Kara Lassen Oliver

Working with the Steering Committee of the United Methodist Youth Organization, I am in a unique position to see and partner with junior highs to develop leadership. The Steering Committee that directs and manages the United Methodist Youth Organization is composed of youth and adults, 75 percent of whom are youth under the age of eighteen. Youth chair all of our committees and have ultimate responsibility for granting money, budgeting, hiring staff, and programs.

One of our greatest assets at the Youth Organization is that we have a twenty-five year history of youth in leadership. Whether youth are attending their first Steering Committee meeting or they are working with staff over the phone or via e-mail, there is a history and established trust and expectation of their leadership skills, not in spite of their being youth, but because they are youth. The goals are for youth to recognize their potential, provide space for growth and development, and for youth to succeed and be affirmed. Adult workers with youth face three challenges in that process.

The first challenge is to be sure that the trust we place in youth is paired with the necessary tools and information that enable youth to make informed and responsible decisions.

While in junior high, Amber (not her real name) served on the Youth Service Fund Project Review Committee (PRC) two years, her second year as chair of that committee. She and her committee were responsible for reading, reviewing, and discussing eighty projects that had been submitted for funding. The committee selects ten to fifteen projects that meet the Youth Service Fund criteria of youth involvement, empowerment, and discipleship. Amber and the other youth on the committee were able to complete this daunting task with competence and integrity because they received training to accomplish the task, were given review sheets that asked them to look for specific assets and red flags, and they were given the permission and time to discuss and ask questions. Reflecting on the selection process of Youth Service Fund projects, junior high youth, may be the most equipped to make the decisions. Since Amber is a junior high youth, she processes best in concrete terms and can make the most effective decisions if she can relate to or understand the experience being presented. If the application does not meet these developmental requirements of a junior high youth, most likely it is not a strong application and will not be funded.

The second challenge is to focus on the process of decision-making and the development of skills, not a particular outcome or decision.

At my first Steering Committee meeting as a staff person, one of the agenda items was to decide whether the group would use Robert's Rules of Order or a discernment model to guide their decision-making. I wanted so badly to interject my comments, insights, and wisdom into the discussion. I would get fidgety and agitated as I watched the discussion begin to turn away from the "right" decision. My colleague continued to remind me that we needed to focus our energies not on their decision, but on their discussion and thoughtful consideration of the issue. As adults and partners in ministry with them, our role is to provide resources, necessary and relevant information, and a variety of methods for exploring all sides of an issue. Junior high youth will be more confident and effective leaders if they are exposed to and can experiment with different processes and models of leadership. If we invite youth to participate in leadership but only affirm them if they come to the same conclusions we have, then we stifle and alienate the leaders vital to our ministries.

The third challenge is to provide boundaries and a framework within which youth can explore and make decisions.

Junior high youth are just beginning to learn and test their critical-thinking skills and develop their verbal skills. Youth are self-conscious about being able to understand issues and express themselves clearly. Therefore they require time, patience, and affirmation as they ask questions and formulate their own thoughts. When developing leadership with junior high youth be sure to provide manageable tasks and projects, do not patronize them for their short attention spans but plan activities recognizing that developmental need, and select projects with a clear end result.

The foundation for leadership development is through creating an environment where junior high youth are trusted and where they have clear and fair expectations. Youth are perceptive and sensitive to the atmosphere in which they find themselves. They will rise to the expectations and opportunities with which they are presented. If you create a developmentally appropriate and empowering atmosphere, much of the process and logistics of leadership will fall into place. Then youth and youth workers labor as partners in ministry to accomplish the goals of recognizing potential, personal growth, and group success.

To learn more about the United Methodist Youth Organization and the Youth Service Fund, go to *www.umyouth.org*.

Chapter 7

Off the Front Porch: Junior Highs and Community

It was a great idea, or so I thought. At the beginning of a new school year, I would gather together the rising eighth graders for a brainstorming session. We would pray together, eat a good home-cooked meal (instead of pizza), and dream up great ideas for the coming year's youth group. The turnout was extraordinary. Seems that the youth had a lot of ideas for things they wanted to do. After a great meal and a Spirit-filled devotion, I stepped up to the flip chart and opened the floodgates. The ideas flowed like a mighty river.

By the end of the night, we had six retreats, three ski-trips, four scavenger hunts, eight different themed lock-ins, and a roller-coaster tour of the East Coast. In addition, we had monthly birthday parties, weekly drop-ins, and an occasional Bible study thrown in to keep me happy (and employed, I guess). After everyone left, I sat dumbfounded staring at the newsprint. I must have looked pretty glum when my wife noticed and came to sit beside me. "Not what you expected, huh," she asked? "Not at all. I was expecting some good ideas for fun things to do, but that wasn't the main purpose. I really wanted to get an idea of what they were really looking for in youth group. Instead, I got a to-do list that would make my grandfather faint." "Did you," she asked, "or did you get an even better sense of what they want out of youth group?" "Huh?" "Well, what do you see on the page? Look behind the ideas and maybe you'll see some answers." "Thanks, Yoda," I thought to myself. "That's helpful."

Long after Diane went to bed for the night I continued to stare at the papers scattered before me. There really was something to all of this mess. Yes, the ideas we had were all fun, exciting, and extremely expensive. But there was a thread running through the pages that tied them all together. But what was it? I went to bed frustrated and woke up startlingly in the middle of the night thinking "community!" I got out of bed and walked downstairs to the scattered pages. Not surprisingly, Diane was right. There was more to all of these ideas than a bunch of random activities. Retreats, lock-ins, parties, even the roller-coaster tour all pointed to the same fundamental yearning of the eighth-grade students—the desire to be connected with a close community of friends.

We've already identified the importance of peers for junior highs. The church should be a place where every young person can feel safe, nurtured, and accepted. The students who sat around my living room were not trying to make a cruise director out of me; they were merely pointing to their need to be accepted, connected, and close. Of course, they wanted all of the adventure-filled trips and the endless parties, but that wasn't the heart of it. In *Sacred Bridges*, Mike Ratliff identified three key needs for senior high youth. The same needs apply for junior highs. Like their counterparts, junior highs are desperately seeking hospitality, community, and intimacy.

Hospitality

A few years ago, Diane and I moved into a new city. For the first time in nine years of married life, neither of us was working for a local church. We were excited about the prospects of "church-shopping" and quickly went about setting a strategy for our visits. At one church, the pastor greeted the congregation and asked visitors to identify themselves. We raised our hands and were given "welcome" buttons by the ushers. When we got to our car, we joked that the buttons must have been a secret symbol meaning "avoid at all cost." The only person that spoke to us was a colleague from my new job who ran from the choir loft to catch us on our way out the door. Needless to say, we didn't return to that church. Instead, we ended up in a community where we were welcomed, shown around the building, and led to the appropriate Sunday school classes.

That was a difficult experience for Diane and me. Imagine what it must be like to be in junior high and encounter a similar situation. For a young person who is struggling to form an identity and dealing with low self-esteem, that kind of experience can be damaging. Unfortunately, too many youth go to churches where they encounter the same inhospitable spirit. At the door, the pastor or another youth leader welcomes them but none of the youth talk to them throughout the night and they leave wondering if anyone cared that they were there. New junior high youth will judge your ministry based on one question — were they welcomed warmly? If the answer is no, it is safe to say that they will not return. Likewise, if young people who are part of your church do not feel that the group is welcoming to outsiders, they will not bring their friends.

Hospitality is primarily about first impressions. How was I welcomed when I came? Were people willing to talk to me? What kind of environment was it? Young people will judge your group based on their first experience before they will be willing to return for more. At the same time, hospitality is not a surface issue. It is not merely a matter of establishing a "welcoming committee" or giving gifts to newcomers. Believe it or not, the hospitality displayed in your church or youth group has a lot to do with how you understand God, how you view the Christian community, and what you feel about evangelism.

When selling a house, the realtor will insist that the yard is meticulous, the flowers in the garden are bloomed and lovely, and the front porch is welcoming. Moving beyond the first impression of pulling in to the driveway is difficult, regardless of what the inside of the house looks like. Creating a welcoming environment involves significant amounts of time, energy, and commitment. Sadly, too many junior high youth ministries focus all of their energy on the inside of the house when many young people will never get beyond the front porch. Here are some ideas to care for your porch:

1. Enlist youth to reach out to newcomers. This does not mean create a welcoming committee. In fact it shouldn't be obvious or even recognizable by most of the young people in the youth group. Instead, quietly find the young people in your group who have the spiritual gift of hospitality and encourage and equip them to use that gift as part of their ministry. There is far more power for a junior high student when a peer spends time talking with them than when ten adults do.

2. Remember names. A lot of people get very defensive when I talk about the importance of names. Many people hide behind excuses like, "I'm not good at remembering names." Well, if you are not good at it—practice! I cannot underscore enough how important it is to junior high students when you remember their name the second time you talk with them. Develop some sort of system to remember the names of new people. When I meet a young person, I will say their name at least five times during our initial conversation even if it is only two-minutes long. That way, I am drilling the name into my memory. It is awkward at first, but it is a great way to remember names.

3. Monitor teasing. We all know that a junior high school can be a pretty rough place. In fact, many of us probably have horrible memories about being teased ourselves. The truth is that what may seem like harmless banter is actually devastating to early adolescents. When a young person attends your youth group, they need to experience an environment that is free of ridicule and full of grace. Make sure that the young people in your group know that you will not tolerate put-downs. Also make sure that you or the other adult leaders do not use sarcasm (literally translated "tearing of the flesh") when relating with one another or the youth in the group.

Community

Once young people enter the front door of your ministry program, they are looking to move into the living room and connect with peers in a safe, nonthreatening atmosphere. Junior high youth desperately need peer groups where they can try on different roles, build confidence, and be themselves.

Youth group can be a great place to help early adolescents develop friendships that cut across the perceived or real boundaries that exist in school. Community is built on common characteristics, likes, and interests. Christian community is centered on the person of Jesus Christ who breaks down barriers and calls us to share with one another in the life of discipleship.

The great thing about community is that it can be built. Community doesn't just happen when some teens show up to your group. Student and adult leaders need to be actively trying to build a sense of community. Dozens of resources are available to help you build community in your group. A must have for building community in youth groups is *Go for It! Games: 25 Faith-Building Adventures for Groups,* by Walt Marcum (Abingdon Press, 1998; ISBN: 0-687-08728-7).

Three easy ideas for building community with junior highs are:

1. **Here comes the herd.** Many junior highs love being together with adult leaders and peers. In addition, young people love to have you attend a concert, play, or sporting event. Combine those two things by having a weekly or monthly outing to one of your students' activities. Load up the church van or your car and bring whoever is available to watch a game or listen to a concert. Give youth an opportunity to sign up to have "the herd" visit their activity.

2. **Create a "slogo."** Every year, ask young people to come up with a new logo and slogan for your youth group. Give them ideas and provide all of the resources they may need (art supplies, computer programs, Scripture verses). Once the slogo has been created, use it to make letterhead, banners, and business cards that young people can use to invite friends to the group. This is a great way to allow the artistic talents in your group to shine and to create a sense of unity in your group.

3. **Initiative games and low ropes courses.** These are more challenging but have always been effective for our junior highs. Before going to a ropes course, be sure that none of the activities are based on skill or athletic ability. In addition, avoid games that will make someone feel uncomfortable about being too tall, too short, or too heavy. Most ropes courses have trained leaders who understand the developmental needs of early adolescents and will help you design the perfect program that fits your group's goals. Don't use that as an excuse to cut short your prep time. Instead, see it as an opportunity to tailor your group's experience to meet their needs.

Intimacy

While building community is an important step in developing an effective junior high ministry, it is not the end of the road. More than being connected with others on the basis of common interests, young people are longing to develop relationships where they can take their masks off and struggle with difficult issues. We need to provide opportunities for junior highs to move beyond an experience of community and enter into the communion of faith. Being in communion with others on this journey means "that we participate in a common life, united by Jesus Christ, and experience the joys and pains of others as though they were our own" (*The Godbearing Life*, 112). We are called to help young people be in communion with others in the Body of Christ. To be a part of a communion requires being willing to forgive one another, to trust one another, to share one another's burdens, and to defer our own desires in the interest of others. Real intimacy happens when we are willing to journey with others in love and practice the faith together.

In a community, junior highs will share their prayer requests. In Holy Communion, they will learn to pray for one another. In community, they will *go to* worship together. In Communion, they *will* worship together. In community, they will *partake* together in the Body and Blood of Christ. In Communion, they will *become* the Body of Christ for one another and the world.

In our house, the living room is the place where we welcome guests and get to know new friends. It is warm and inviting with plenty of places for everyone to sit comfortably. The family room is where we invite people to share in the messiness of our lives. Toys are scattered everywhere, the television is usually on, and the children run freely. While we can *make* friends in the living room, we can *be* friends in the family room. The same is true for junior high youth ministry. Young people come into our groups and are welcomed into the living room where we build community and make friends. Unfortunately, many groups never move beyond the living room and into the family room where young people can share their deepest hurts and frustrations, wrestle with difficult issues in a safe environment, and be nurtured in their faith journey.

While living rooms often take on the look of a designer magazine, family rooms are usually disheveled and intimate, reflecting the characteristics of the family that lives there. Similarly, your group needs to develop communion in a way that fits the values of your church and community. While there are no "how-to" books for building communion in your junior high group, I have found some effective ways to develop intimacy among junior highs.

- **Build a covenant.** To be able to remove their masks and develop intimate relationships with peers and adults, young people need to trust that they will be safe and accepted. One way to create a safe environment is to build a group covenant. More than a set of do's and don'ts, a covenant is a promise made between two or more parties and God. Ask young people to identify things that are necessary for them to feel comfortable to be themselves. Then ask members of the youth group to sign the covenant and post it in a prominent spot. The last junior high covenant that my group developed included: use words that can build you up, not tear you down; every prayer concern is confidential; laughter is healthy, but not when it comes at someone else's expense; and be yourself.

Use small groups. Small groups are a necessary aspect of junior high youth ministry. Most young people who are struggling with identity formation and negative self-image will not feel comfortable sharing in a large group setting. Wherever possible, provide small groups for young people to pray together, study the Bible, and do service projects together. In many cases, same-sex groups are most effective for junior highs because the developmental differences and the issues confronting boys and girls in early adolescence are drastically different. However, it is also important to provide opportunities for young people to develop healthy relationships with members of the opposite sex.

Have prayer partners. Encourage young people to take their friendships to a deeper level by forming prayer partners. With junior highs, it will probably not work to pull names out of a hat or randomly assign prayer partners. Rather, ask young people to form themselves into pairs or groups and have them "register" as prayer partners. Develop a list of prayer concerns for the church, the community, and the world. Assign each group two or three things to pray for during each meeting and ask them to take turns praying. Because they are with their friends, they will be more comfortable than if they were with others that they did not know as well. In time, these prayer groups will be more comfortable sharing their own concerns and praying for one another.

Hospitality, community, intimacy—all three are important needs of junior highs. However, be careful not to assume that all young people are ready for the deepest level of friendship. The funnel is a popular model for youth ministry that has been used to describe the different communities of young people in your sphere of influence. The same model can be used to look at the intimacy needs of junior high young people.

- Hospitality: What would a young person experience if she came to your youth group for the first time? Would she be welcomed? Would she feel comfortable? Would she want to return? Creating a hospitable atmosphere is making sure that all young people—whether they are members, friends, or visitors—feel welcomed into your group.
- Community: This is the level where most young people in your group will feel comfortable. Community is a safe place where young people

can feel accepted, develop strong peer relationships, and experience the Body of Christ. We can and should take every opportunity to help young people connect with one another and form community.

- Intimacy: This is the level where a group moves beyond community and enters into communion. You probably have a small number of young people who are ready for the intimacy that comes with being in communion with others. Provide opportunities for people to develop more intimate relationships with one another, but do not force closeness.

Chapter 8

Crazy, Called, and Committed: The Junior High Youth Worker

I am sure that all of us have dreamed it at one point or another. You move to the front of the sanctuary at the beginning of the program year to ask for volunteers for the junior high ministry. After an emotional, heart-felt plea nine people stand up to respond to the call to this particular ministry. After worship, these new recruits crowd into the youth room and hang on every word as you line out the program for the coming year.

Unfortunately for most of us, this is a dream. Whether you are a pastor, Christian educator, youth leader, or parent responsible for the junior high youth program at your church, chances are you've faced the dilemma of recruiting volunteers to support this ministry. The truth is that junior high ministry frightens most people. I'm sure you've heard it all before. "I don't relate well to junior highs—they're too emotional." "I'm better working with people who don't have all of that energy." "I'd rather work with teenagers who are more ready for spiritual input." "I'd rather have root canal every Sunday."

Sadly, many youth ministry resources heighten this fear by making a constant string of jokes and misstatements about junior high ministry. In almost every conference that I have attended on youth ministry there are repeated jokes about junior high youth. In a recent edition of a journal for youth ministry professionals, two cartoons portrayed the same negative stereotyping that junior high youth ministers often struggle against. The gist of the first is a soldier standing in front of a military review board and responding to a question on terrorism. "Terrorist experience? Yes Sirs! I taught junior high Sunday school back home!" In the second, the image is a preacher delivering a sermon, . . . "and so, as Paul said in the Bible, he fought wild beasts. . . . " In the congregation one man turns to another and says, "Sounds like Paul was a junior high minister." Is it any wonder why people steer clear of junior high youth ministry?

Crazy, Called, and Committed

How to Recruit

Break down myths and alleviate fears: It's true. Many adults are afraid of junior high students. The reality is that junior high ministry can be very scary. However, it can also be argued that junior high ministry is the most important ministry of the church. The first step in recruiting volunteers for junior high youth ministry is breaking down prevailing myths of junior high youth ministry and lessening fears and misconceptions.

Myth 1: Junior high youth are disrespectful and uncontrollable.

The truth is that junior high youth are highly respectful of authority. When rules and covenants for behavior are clearly established junior high youth tend to act in accordance with those expectations. Developmentally, junior high youth want to please adults in their lives and conformity to rules is one way to do that. That is not to say that you won't have problems arise or students that will push the boundaries.

Myth 2: Junior high youth ministry is all fun and games.

It is true that junior high ministry must be highly active and constantly in motion in order to keep students interested. It is also true that junior high students are. Junior highs are still forming their value systems and shaping their identities. Junior high ministry must engage young people spiritually and provide significant opportunities for young people to encounter Jesus Christ.

Myth 3: Junior highs don't want adults around.

This myth is perhaps the furthest from the truth. Every junior high young person that I have met is craving the attention and care of adults. Because of the overwhelming rate of change happening to their bodies and minds, junior high youth want the stability that comes from relationships with significant adults.

Before you even begin recruiting volunteers, begin with educating the congregation about what your junior high ministry is all about. Allow them to hear from junior high students who return from a retreat fired up about their faith. Ask them to pray for the junior high students by name and involve students in other ministries of the church. Give them opportunities to read about your philosophy of junior high ministry in the church newsletter and bulletin. The best thing you can do in recruiting is preemptively strike down common myths and misunderstandings about who early adolescents are and what junior high ministry is all about. Help the congregation understand the importance of junior high ministry and the role of the entire church in nurturing the spiritual development of young people.

Promise and deliver training and support. Perhaps the greatest fear that adults face when asked to consider junior high ministry is that they are ill prepared for the task. On the surface, many adults will respond to a call to participate in junior high ministry by pointing to fears about junior high students. In many cases the truth is that they are not afraid of junior highs as much as they feel inadequate for the responsibility. The surest way to reduce these feelings of inadequacy is to promise and deliver quality guidance and training. Unfortunately, in many cases, we find people willing to take on the task of junior high youth ministry and we sit them in a room with fifteen early adolescents and a book or curriculum. Effective training for junior high ministry should be:

- Theological: At the beginning of this book, I laid out my theology for junior high ministry that is built around a Wesleyan understanding of grace. Training adults to lead junior high ministry programs must begin with communicating your theological understanding of junior high ministry and the desired spiritual outcomes of student involvement. A junior high ministry program that is not theologically grounded will easily succumb to the danger of trying to attract youth solely on the basis of fun and games. Adult leaders must understand the goal of your ministry and discover how they fit in to the overall missional strategy.
- Instructional: An essential part of effective training for junior high ministry is helping adults understand who junior highs are. Training should include an overview of the physical, emotional, intellectual, social, and spiritual development of early adolescents. In order to counter the perceived myths about junior highs, adults must have a realistic understanding of where they are in their developmental process. In addition, it is important to help adults have an understanding of the cultural patterns of early adolescents.
- Practical: Another fear that prospective volunteers have is that they will have no idea what to actually do with students in a youth meeting or Sunday school class. Provide them with resources and materials that you have tested and found to be effective with junior highs. Help teachers and leaders understand how junior highs learn; assist them in using appropriate and creative learning techniques.

In addition to training, show strong support for those adults working in junior high ministry. Too often, adults are recruited to lead youth programs and then pushed off the plank into the deep waters of ministry to swim on their own. Nothing is more frustrating for volunteers in junior high ministry than to feel as if the have been roped into something and then left to fend for themselves. A good friend of mine had been volunteering with junior high ministry at his church for more than ten years when a staff person challenged him about using the "staff only" photocopier in the church office. Not only was he frustrated about the lack of courtesy displayed by the staff person, but also he was annoyed that he was entitled to be around young people who were at a crucial point in their faith development but not allowed to use a copy machine. At that point he felt little or no support from the people who had asked him to serve in this ministry role and he thought seriously about giving up.

Involve young people in recruiting. Not surprisingly, young people have a lot to say about the things they are looking for in a youth leader. You may be surprised, however, at what they have to say. In a survey conducted by Mike Nappa, young people ranked the qualities that they found most desirable in adult volunteers for youth ministry. The number one quality that youth are looking for in leaders is a commitment to Jesus Christ. More than 44 percent of young people listed that as their number one concern. Second, young people were looking for adults with a "caring attitude" that would accept them and love them. The third ranked characteristic, before we get too mushy, is fun. Junior high young people crave relationships with adults who can have fun and enjoy life. More important, they want to know that the Christian life is full of joy and zeal (*What I Wish My Youth Leader Knew About Youth Ministry*, 187).

It may also surprise you to discover what young people do not care about in the selection of volunteer leaders. Generally, young people do not care about the age or teaching ability of the volunteers. Contrary to the "guitar playing, athletic, attractive, and young" stereotype of successful youth leaders, young people are much more interested in how much adult leaders love God and love them.

I will never forget Dennis and Peachy Wood. They were a retired couple, well into their seventies, when I joined the junior high youth group at my church. Every week, Dennis would show up to youth group in a polyester suit and Peachy would be in a long dress. They were anything but "cool" by our standards. In fact, the first few times I was there I was determined to make fun of them to gain the laughter and approval of my peers. Whenever I caused trouble Dennis would come and sit down beside me and put his arm on my shoulder. "Drew," he would say, "one of these days you are going to know why it is important to listen. When that day comes, I will be right here beside you." Every Friday morning Dennis and Peachy would walk by my bus stop just to say hello. When it was cold, they would bring me hot chocolate. Once in a while they would bring cookies for me to share with my friends. And, sure enough, when I decided to commit my life to Jesus Christ on a junior high retreat, Dennis was sitting right beside me with his arm on my shoulder.

When asked, young people will have numerous suggestions of adults in your congregation who treat them with love and respect, exhibit a deep faith, and know how to have fun. Not only can they help identify possible volunteers, they can also be the best recruiters. After your young people have identified potential leaders, work with them to develop a strategy for getting them involved. A friend recently told me that his junior high students threw a Pentecost party and invited people that they thought would make great volunteers. During the party, different students would go to the microphone and talk about how the youth group had impacted their life. Toward the end of the evening one eighth grader talked about the birth of the church in Acts and the role that every Christian has in continuing the ministry of Christ in the world. She then invited the adults at the party to consider being a part of the junior high ministry in the coming year. The response to the invitation was phenomenal.

Whom to Recruit

Now that you have some ideas about how to go about recruiting adult volunteers, it is important to understand who you are looking for. Building on the characteristics generated by the young people in Nappa's survey, I identify five key traits that you should look for in adult volunteers for junior high ministry:

Adults who love junior highs. Of course, most adults are not going to jump up and say that out of any age group, junior highs are their all-time favorite to work with. If you can find those people, hang on to them and don't let go. If they are not banging down your doors, there are ways that you can identify them. One of the easiest ways to do that is to watch adult interaction with junior highs. During coffee hour, after worship services, in the hallways, pay attention to the way that different adults interact with junior high students. Chances are that if you can sense a noticeable disdain in a look or verbal interaction between an adult and a junior high student, they won't be your first targets. However, if you notice someone who is always friendly and takes time to speak directly to a young person you may want to consider asking him or her.

Adults who love God. Commitment to Christ is the first thing that young people are looking for in adult leaders. This priority does not mean that everyone working with the junior high youth ministry at your church must be a spiritual giant who spends two or more hours a day in prayer and reads his or her Bible daily. Just like students, adults are on a journey of faith and we know that sanctification is a lifelong process. Junior high youth are not looking for spiritual experts, they are looking for spiritual people. They are not looking for adults who will have all of the answers; they are looking for adults who will listen to their questions. Young people need to be surrounded by adults who are at different points on their faith journey who are actively seeking to grow spiritually.

Adults with time to invest. Early adolescents are hungering for the attention and involvement of adults in their lives. Junior highs need adults who are willing and able to be involved in their lives both inside and outside of the church. One of the foundational tenets of youth ministry is that the gospel is communicated most effectively through significant relationships among youth and adults. Paul writes to the church at Thessalonica, "We loved you so much that we were delighted to share with you not only the gospel of God but our lives as well, because you had become so dear to us" (1 Thessalonians 2:8, NIV) The most effective outreach to junior high students is relational. Junior highs need adults who are willing to open up their lives and share their hearts with young people. They need adults who will take the time to get to know them as individuals and journey with them on the path of spiritual growth.

> *Junior high youth are not looking for spiritual experts, they are looking for spiritual people.*

Adults who are caring, patient, and loving. Junior high youth need to feel safe, loved, and nurtured by adults. That said, chances are that they will test every adult who shows interest in them. Junior highs will break rules, act up, and push the limits of your patience in order to know that you really mean what you say about love and forgiveness. They want to know that you will love them unconditionally and many junior highs will push you to prove it. Adult leaders must also be patient because they will generally not see the same kind of results typically associated with success. Rarely will a young teen stop to tell you how important you are to them or how much you mean in their lives. Rather, they will ignore e-mails, not return phone calls, and pretend they don't know you in the mall. However, by constantly reaffirming your unconditional love for them and God's love for them, you will be planting seeds that may not grow for years to come. The junior high youth worker must be willing to water the ground and not necessarily see the harvest.

Adults who are comfortable being adults. My worst experience with junior high youth workers is when adults try to "be" junior highs. The fact is that junior high students are not looking for adults who want to be their peers. The best junior high youth worker can be fun loving, creative, and even goofy at times while also being someone who young people will turn to when crisis comes to their family or their faith is shaken. Young people need the stability that comes from caring adults who are comfortable with who they are and do not feel the need to go out of their way to impress them.

The bottom line for adults who work with junior high youth is this: love God, love youth. Nothing can be simpler or more effective. All of the training in the world cannot equal that simple formula for successful junior high ministry. When we are able to put these first things first, the rest of the story will fall into place.

Supporting Volunteers in Youth Ministry

by Lynne Wells Graziano

As a veteran volunteer youth worker, I have had the privilege of working alongside excellent youth leaders and youth ministers. From them I've not only learned a tremendous amount about ministry, but I have also identified the key ideals for volunteer growth, satisfaction, and longevity:

Treat me as an equal. I respect the level of education and training you bring to the program and I know that I haven't attended seminary, graduated from a youth ministry program, or even been to the number of training courses you have attended. But the Bible promises that in Christ there is equality, so I ask for your respect of my faith, my love, and my desire to serve God by working with youth. Ask my opinion on significant issues, not just on what type of food to serve Sunday night. Challenge me to find an answer in Scripture to a question the kids have been kicking around. Let me know that something I shared with the group spoke to you, not just the youth.

Communicate without ceasing. Communication is the key to any successful relationship. Hopefully you wouldn't expect your spouse, or children, or senior pastor to anticipate your every need and desire; please don't expect me to either. More than even the youth or the parents, I need to know the schedule of upcoming events, the costs involved, the numbers you anticipate, and the role you have chosen for me. In return, I will communicate with you regarding my availability, my limitations, and my willingness to serve where assigned.

Train me and teach me. Even though I am not drawing a monetary paycheck, I like to be included in professional growth and training opportunities. Have you read a good book recently that has shaped your thinking or challenged you spiritually? Pass it on to me. Are you attending a seminar or workshop for youth workers? Let me tag along; better yet, encourage me to tag along by defraying the expenses involved! Open up your library of tapes, videos, magazines, and other professional materials that will make me both a better volunteer and a stronger Christian.

Crazy, Called, and Committed

Challenge my comfort zone. What kind of a leader will I be if I am never willing to try something new or move beyond the comfortable? Just as Jesus challenged his disciples, you need to constantly push me to think and act outside the established borders of my life. Help me arrange my family obligations so that I can get away on a service project with the youth. Ask me to set up a program for the youth to help at the local food bank. Push me to prepare a presentation for the church staff. Make me responsible for the fund-raising project, even if I can't balance a checkbook! Allow me the privilege of taking a leap of faith for a God that will not fail me.

Allow me to innovate and initiate. Most youth pastors or leaders would love a group of volunteers that step up and take charge, but the environment for innovation and initiative is established and encouraged by your leadership. If I say, "I think we should serve our community as a group," you should say, "I'll give you a date and a time that is open for you to set up a service night." Then let me set it up, even if it's not perfect! If I come up with a crazy idea for a lock-in, let me run with it (as long as I promise to actually be there for the event). If I want to put aside the Sunday school curriculum for a special program or activity, trust my abilities enough to know I'll still be "teaching," but in a different fashion.

Recognize and reward my commitment. I am a volunteer committed to youth, but I won't last forever with cold pizza and warm sodas as my only reward. Allow me the flexibility of a night off when my family needs me at home, remember to thank my spouse for the silent support and behind-the-scenes encouragement. Realize that as much as I love these kids, I need some time for my own. Plan a party for volunteers and their spouses: a party we don't have to plan or clean up after. Ask the kids to provide occasional free or inexpensive babysitting so that my husband and I can have a night out. Allow me, and the other volunteers, to share in your youth ministry triumphs.

Love me and accept me, just as I am. You can preach unconditional love to the youth, but you teach it when you model it. I have mostly good days occasionally marred by cranky moods or fragile moments. Love me through them all, even when you might not like me very much. Your love and encouragement nurtures my own desire to model the love of Jesus to all of God's children. Together we can set a tone of caring and acceptance for everyone.

Be a prayer partner. Youth ministry can be exhausting, leaving us vulnerable to frustration and temptation. I want to pray for you and bring your concerns to the Lord, and ask that you do the same for me. Prayer time with our leadership team will cement the bonds between us and strengthen us in our service. Let's agree to pray before each event, literally placing our work into the hands of God.

Chapter 9
Love God—Love Teens

I'm sure that we have all heard of the KISS principle—keep it simple, stupid. As I was developing this book, one of my great friends and mentors reminded me of this principle. After he read my outline, he cautioned me: "Don't let your book create a formula for junior high ministry that replaces your passionate commitment to love young people into the kingdom of God." He was right. I hope that as you read these pages you discovered (or uncovered) your own theological framework for your junior high ministry. I hope that you learned helpful information about early adolescent development and characteristics of the millennial generation. I trust that you wrestled with issues of spiritual formation and leadership development. But most important, I pray that you found fuel to ignite your passion for the ministry of loving junior high students.

Junior high ministry boils down to a very simple formula: love God, love teens. In order to be effective in junior high ministry, you must be growing in your own understanding of the Christian faith. More important, you must be striving to live out the faith in your daily life. Like it or not, junior high youth are not listening to your lessons as much as they are listening to your life. Early adolescents have incredible radar and can detect when they are hearing words off a page instead of from the heart. Being authentic in ministry means that you are sharing your own faith journey—mountaintops and valleys— with those with whom you are walking.

The second part to that formula is to love kids unconditionally. Whether they break the rules or break your heart, love them. When they fail to fulfill their promises, love them. When they make you so angry that you could cry, love them. When they ruin your plans and wreck your office, love them. The old adage is true—people don't care how much you know until they know how much you care. Junior high youth won't care about your lessons or your programs unless they know that they are loved and accepted for who they are.

When I remember the people who were most influential in my spiritual development in junior high, they had two things in common: They loved God and they loved me. It was not their ability to play the guitar or their wizardry on the basketball court that drew me in. It was their faith that shined through everything that they did and their love that never gave up on me. It was Dennis and Peachy Wood, the retired couple who was always at youth group and visited me at my bus stop. It was Dale Irvin, my first youth pastor who loved me even when I didn't love myself. It was Rich Hendrickson, a friend and mentor who welcomed me into his family and shared his life.

As you enter into the messy world of junior high ministry, remember this simple formula. More than any book, curriculum, or retreat, this formula will shape your ministry and ensure your success. Remember, under all of the particulars there lays a passion. Keep it simple: love God; love teens. The rest is details.

Appendix 1
Early Adolescent Development Resources

- *The Secret Life of the Brain,* by Richard Restak (Joseph Henry Press, 2000) ISBN 0-309-07435-5.

- *Inside the Brain: Revolutionary Discoveries of How the Mind Works,* by Ronald Kotulak (Andrews McMeel Publishing, 1997) ISBN: 0-836-23289-5.

- *"Inside the Teenage Brain,"* (Frontline PBS video) Item Number: FRL92012.

- *Lifespan Human Development,* 6th ed., by Anne V. Gormly (Harcourt Brace College Publishers, 1997) Item Code: FROL2012

- *The Adolescent Experience,* 4th ed., by Thomas P. Gullotta, Gerald R. Adams, Carol A. Markstrom (Academic Press, 2000) ISBN: 0-12-305560-1 .

- *Healthy Teen: Facing the Challenges of Young Lives,* 3rd ed., by Alice R. McCarthy (Bridge Communications, 2000) ISBN: 0-9621645-5-0.

- *Our Last Best Shot: Guiding Our Children Through Early Adolescence,* by Laura Sessions Stepp (Riverhead Books, 2000) ISBN: .

- *Adolescence: Continuity, Change, and Diversity,* by Nancy J. Cobb (Mayfield Publishing, 1992) ISBN: 0767416872.

- *Reviving Ophelia: Saving the Selves of Adolescent Girls,* by Mary Bray Pipher (Ballantine Books, 1994) ISBN: 0345418786.

- *Real Boys: Rescuing Our Sons from the Myths of Boyhood,* by William Pollack (Henry Holt & Co., 1999) ISBN: 0805061835.

- *What Teens Need to Succeed: Proven, Practical Ways to Shape Your Own Future,* by Peter L. Benson, Judy Galbraith, and Pamela Espeland (Free Spirit Publishing, 1997) ISBN: 1575420279.

- *Raising Cain: Protecting the Emotional Life of Boys,* by Dan Kindlon and Michael Thompson (Ballantine Books, 1999) ISBN: 0345434854 .

General Youth Ministry Resources

- *The Godbearing Life: The Art of Soul Tending for Youth Ministry,* by Kenda Creasy Dean and Ron Foster (Upper Room Books, 1998) ISBN: 0835808580.

- *When Kumbaya Is Not Enough: A Practical Theology for Youth Ministry,* by Dean Borgman (Hendrickson Publishers, 1997) ISBN: 1565632478.

- *The Ministry of Nurture: A Youth Worker's Guide to Discipling Teenagers,* by Duffy Robbins (Zondervan, 1990) ISBN: 0310525810.

- *Claiming the Name: A Theological and Practical Overview of Confirmation,* by John Gooch (Abingdon Press, 2000) ISBN: 080662311X.

- *Youthwork and the Mission of God: Frameworks for Relational Outreach,* by Pete Ward (SPCK Publishers, 1997) ISBN: 0281050449.

- *Teaching the Bible Creatively: How to Awaken Your Kids to Scripture,* by Bill McNabb and Steven Mabry (Zondervan, 1990) ISBN: 0310529212.

- *Deepening Youth Spirituality: The Youth Worker's Guide* by Walt Marcum (Abingdon Press, 2001) 0687097258.

- *Starting Right: Thinking Theologically about Youth Ministry,* edited by Kenda Creasy Dean, Chap Clark, and Dave Rahn (Zondervan, 2001) ISBN: 0-310-23406-9.

- *Youth Leadership: A Guide to Understanding Leadership Development in Adolescents,* by Josephine A. Van Linden and Carl I. Fertman (Jossey-Bass Publisher, 1998) ISBN: 0-7879-4059-3.

- *Millennials Rising: The Next Great Generation,* by Neil Howe and William Strauss (Vintage Books, 2001) ISBN: 0375707190 .

- *Postmodern Youth Ministry,* by Tony Jones (Zondervan, 2001) ISBN: 031023817X.

- *Real Teens: A Contemporary Snapshot of Youth Culture,* by George Barna (Regal Books, 2001) ISBN: 0830726632.

- *Twists of Faith: Ministry With Youth at the Turning Points of Their Lives,* by Marcy Balcomb and Kevin Witt (Discipleship Resources, 1999) ISBN: 0881772518.

- *Big Differences: How to Deal With Youth of Various Ages* (Abingdon Press, 1998) ISBN: 0687087600.

Junior High Ministry Resources

- Curriculum Series: *Faith in Motion,* by various authors (Abingdon Press, 2002–2003).

- Curriculum Series: *Bible Quest,* Grades 6–8, by various authors (Bible Quest Publishers, 2003).

- Curriculum Series: *Wild Truth Bible Lessons,* by Mark Oestreicher (Zondervan, 1996) ISBN: 0-310-21304-5.

- *Junior High Ministry: A Guide to Early Adolescence for Youth Workers,* by Wayne Rice (Zondervan, 1998) ISBN: 0-310-22442-X.

- *Way to Live: Christian Practices for Teens,* edited by Dorothy C. Bass and Don C. Richter (Upper Room Books, 2001) ISBN: 0835809757.

- *Go for It! Games: 25 Faith-Building Adventures for Groups* by Walt Marcum (Abingdon Press, 1998) ISBN 0687087287.

- *Big Differences: How to Deal With Youth of Various Ages,* from the Skillabilities series (Abingdon Press, 1998) ISBN: 0687087600.

- *Training Youth for Dynamic Leadership* (Group Publishing, 1999) ISBN: 0764420747.

- *The Justice Mission,* by Jim Hancock (Zondervan, 2002) ISBN: 0-310-24255-X.

- *Creative Junior High Programs from A to Z,* volumes. I and II, by Steve Dickie and Darrell Pearson (Zondervan, 1996) ISBN: 0-310-20779-7.

- *Help, I'm a Junior High Youth Worker,* by Mark Oestreicher (Zondervan, 1997) ISBN:0-310-21328-2.

- *Junior High Game Nights,* by Dan McCollam and Keith Betts, (Zondervan, 1991) 0-310-53811-4.

- *More Junior High Game Nights,* by Dan McCollam and Keith Betts, (Zondervan, 1992) ISBN: 0-310-54101-8.

- *Preteen Worker's Encyclopedia of Bible-Teaching Ideas*: New Testament (Group Publishing, 2002) ISBN: 0764424254.

Web Sites

www.ileadyouth.com
www.youthspecialties.com
www.youthministry.com
www.egadideas.com

www.thesourcefym.com
www.youthpastor.com
www.youthworkers.net

Appendix 2
Top 20 List of Fun Ideas for Junior High Ministry

Bag Skits: Fill a paper bag with random items found around your office or your garage. Try to make sure that the items are not connected or don't provide a natural theme. Divide the group into teams of four or five and have them create a skit based on the Scripture lesson. The trick is that they have to creatively incorporate every item in the bag into their skit.

GNO: Girls and guys night out is a great way to give the guys or girls in the group an opportunity to get together and build relationships with one another and the adult leaders. This usually works best when it is "planned spontaneity." If you are doing a guys night out, find a night that works for all of your male advisors. Split up the list of boys in the group (depending on group size, you may do one grade or the whole group) and make phone call invitations to everyone on the list. You'll have a great time with whatever activity you do but you will also have a natural opportunity to talk about some pressing issues.

Night Worms: This is an idea that usually only works in the summer or during another vacation from school because everyone needs a day to prepare and a day to recover. Plan a normal three-day retreat, except reverse the times. Have everyone stay up as late as they possibly can the night before. (Be sure to tell parents what you are doing.) Arrive at camp early and have everyone go to sleep immediately after an early dinner (4:00 or 5:00). Wake the group up at midnight for breakfast and start your day. Follow a normal retreat schedule with devotions, meals, snacks, free time, and games.

Encouraging Words: Find creative ways to encourage the young people in your group. Some ideas include: writing notes for parents to pack in a lunch; recording your voice on a tape or CD that you mail to the student; cut out letters from the newspaper to send an anonymous note; mow a simple message in their front lawn (be sure you have the parent's permission); shave their name in your head (just kidding—I wanted to be sure you were paying attention).

Scavenger Hunts: Find new ways to put a twist on a classic game. Our groups' favorite was the video scavenger hunt. Each group would get a video camera and go around to different sites to perform activities such as: make a human pyramid on the front lawn of the municipal building; go to a children's playground and ride the merry-go-round; go to the local doughnut shop and videotape the clerk eating a donut; find the pastor and tape your group sleeping while she preaches a sermon in her pajamas (and robe). Of course, you need to make sure all of the businesses, individuals, and the police department know what you are doing in advance.

Stations of the Cross: Each Lenten season we would bring the junior high group to a Catholic retreat center where we would lead them through the Stations of the Cross. It was a great way to focus on the season and learn about another tradition. The nuns at the retreat center would answer questions and provide hot chocolate and cookies afterward.

E-mail Updates: Every week, send out an e-mail update to your group that includes coming events, prayer concerns, and other useful information. Include the parents and adult leaders on the list. It is a great way to keep people informed and connected. For students who don't have e-mail access, find a way to print out the e-mail and deliver it to them.

Halloween Madness: Every year at Halloween, we took the group to a farm owned by a member of the church. We would decorate the barn and prepare a haunted house. It was a great way to involve the senior high group as well. We would play goofy games, have a pumpkin carving contest, serve dinner, and go on a hayride through the fields.

Movie Star: Many junior highs love to see themselves on television. Split the group into teams and have them do skits or interviews based on the lesson. Use a video camera to record the different groups. At the end of the night, play the tape for the whole group. Better yet—save the tapes for the senior graduation banquet! Our youth loved seeing themselves at church five and six years earlier!

Progressive Dinner: The traditional progressive dinner works great. You can have parents provide the different courses and you provide different activities for each stop. Many students love to have the group in their house. It is also fun to add a twist to the traditional concept. We have tried fast-food progressive dinners, dessert-only progressive dinners, and reverse progressive dinners.

Gutter Sundae: Purchase a gutter at your local hardware store. Line the gutter with plastic wrap and fill it with vanilla and chocolate ice cream. Everyone brings in their favorite toppings and piles them on. Top it off with whipped cream and have everyone dig in!

Surprise Wake-up Call: Rent or borrow a costume from a costume shop (we've used a gorilla, Barney®, and a Teletubby®). Contact the parents of students and arrange to wake them up early on a Saturday morning. Have another leader videotape the wake-up calls. After editing the videos (you don't want to embarrass anyone), show them to the group on a Sunday night.

Mystery Night: This tradition started because I couldn't think of what to put in a newsletter for a particular Sunday night so I just put "mystery night." Earlier in the week we called everyone and had them come dressed up for our dinner outing. When everyone arrived in suits and dresses, we piled in the van and went to Burger King. They were surprised by a group of parents who had decorated with lace tablecloths, candles, and real china. The food wasn't that great, but the memories were! Another take on mystery night is to go some place that represents the lesson. For instance, go to a local track and have a lesson about training for the race of faith. See more great ideas in *Destination Unknown: 50 Great Mystery Trips for Youth Groups,* by Sam Halverson (Abingdon Press, 2001; ISBN: 068709724X).

Parent/Youth Supper: Every fall we would have a potluck supper and invite all of the parents to join their children at youth group. After dinner we would play family-themed games and have table discussions. Then we would have time to meet with the parents and go over our philosophy for the junior high ministry and our upcoming program schedule. We would also answer questions and invite parents to pray with one another for their children and the youth ministry.

Manhunt: Let's face it, there are a million ways to play manhunt. Truth be told, I don't even know how to play. I usually make up a quick set of rules and have everyone go play! Regardless, it is one of the young people's favorite games. The basic idea is hide and seek in teams—just make it up as you go!

Family Groups: On every retreat and service project, we would break the group up into small groups called "family groups." These groups would meet several times throughout the day for quick talks, prayer time, and devotions. They would also be discussion groups for the lessons and work groups for meal preparation and clean-up. Most groups would pick a family name and assign roles to everyone in the group.

Drop-in Night: Twice a month, have a drop-in night at someone's home. The idea is for there to be no program or activities. Young people can bring homework, watch television, or play games. It is a great way to invite young people into your home or give them a chance to host the group in their home.

Nursing Home Outreach: I have always been surprised at how well most junior highs do at nursing homes. We have had groups prepare a party for the residents, lead a worship service, or do clown ministry.

Mall Madness: Every Christmas we would take the group to the local mall for the day. We would shop for our families/friends, eat lunch together, and take in a holiday movie. We would also buy gifts for the community angel tree. At the end of the day we would return to the church to eat pizza (yes, we eat pizza) and wrap our gifts.

And, of course, my all time favorite...

The "I Couldn't Have Planned This if I'd Tried" Event: On our way to a winter retreat in the mountains, we got stuck in a driving snowstorm. About two hours into the trip, one of the cars got stuck trying to go up a hill. We determined that we couldn't make it up the mountain and we would have to turn back. Quickly, I called the local United Methodist church and tracked down the pastor at her home. I explained the situation and she opened up the church for us to sleep on the floors. The group had so much fun that they decided that they would rather stay another night than drive up the mountain. The pastor agreed and we joined the local congregation for worship on Sunday morning. Without a doubt, this was the retreat that students talk about to this day. You may not be able to plan a snowstorm, but you can plan for a mix-up to change your plans completely. Another time we got in the vans to go to another church for a youth rally. I advertised for weeks and the youth were pumped. When we arrived at the other church, the youth leader greeted us and told us that the rally was last week. She invited us in and we joined her youth group for a great night of food, fellowship, and Bible study.